Introduction

Most cities have guidebooks describing their activities, listing theaters, museums, restaurants, hotels, and special events of interest to tourists. For a few cities there are guidebooks to significant architecture. In both cases activities and architecture are presented as objects within the city to be searched out and enjoyed.

This book does not try to duplicate traditional guides to Philadelphia. It is a guide to the physical environment of the city, presented in the way visitors and citizens see and experience it. Most people move through the city by car or on foot. Thus the views along streets or walkways, rather than views of isolated buildings, create the image of the city.

The material in this book has been selected with both the general visitor and architecturally oriented visitor in mind. Each portion of the book provides general information about the historic background of the city—its present forms and activities—and uses architecture as visual landmarks to help identify specific locations and areas. The maps have been designed for easy understanding yet contain complete locational information for all significant buildings in the city. For those with architectural interests, the index to these buildings includes names of architects and dates of construction.

The first two sections of the book comprise a guide to the city following major routes and key areas. The routes selected are those most used by both visitor and resident. Typical views and significant buildings that serve as visual landmarks are presented in the context in which they are seen. From these routes key areas of generally homogeneous land use extend outward. Areas representative of the key sections of other cities have been selected such as major parks and downtown, university, historic, and residential sections.

The third section of the book describes the historic patterns of growth and the regional context. The growth of Philadelphia from the landing of William Penn to the present is traced in terms of population, urbanization, and location of ethnic settlements. Significant political and legal information of interest to the visitor is also provided. Places of interest throughout the region such as museums, parks, or historic sites are described in relation to their historical development and to transportation systems.

The last section of the book is of more specific interest to architects. It includes some of the key historic plans developed to guide the growth of the city as well as selected examples of architecture, past and present. The descriptions of outstanding interior design should be of interest to professional and general visitor alike.

Routes

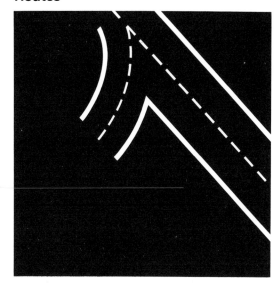

Public streets are the primary determinants of the form of the city. They range in scale from expressways, to major arterial streets, and to smaller streets characteristic of a particular area of the city. Certain buildings stand out along the routes, either by position or architectural appearance, and usually serve as visual landmarks that help to identify specific places or characteristics of specific areas. The routes and the physical environment along them are the initial and dominant experience of the city for all people.

Areas

Housing, commerce, and industry all expand along movement systems. These areas invariably touch on the major routes of the city and then grow out from them into fairly well defined areas of consistent use. Within most cities there are a limited number of areas of particular interest—downtown, universities, primary residential areas—each with its own architectural environment.

Bus System

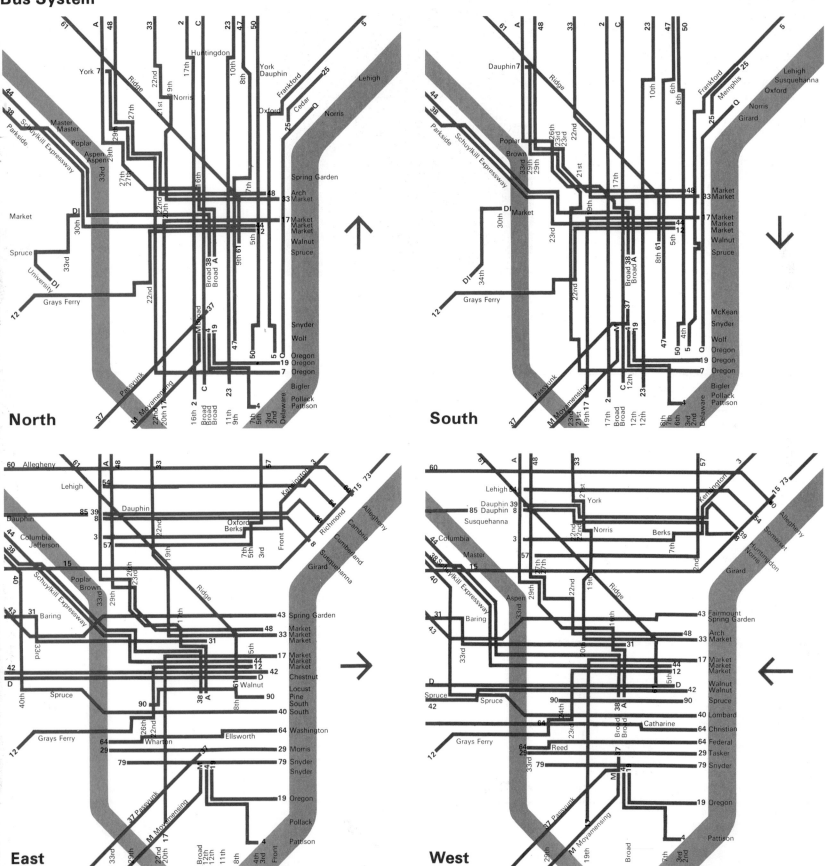

North

South

East

West

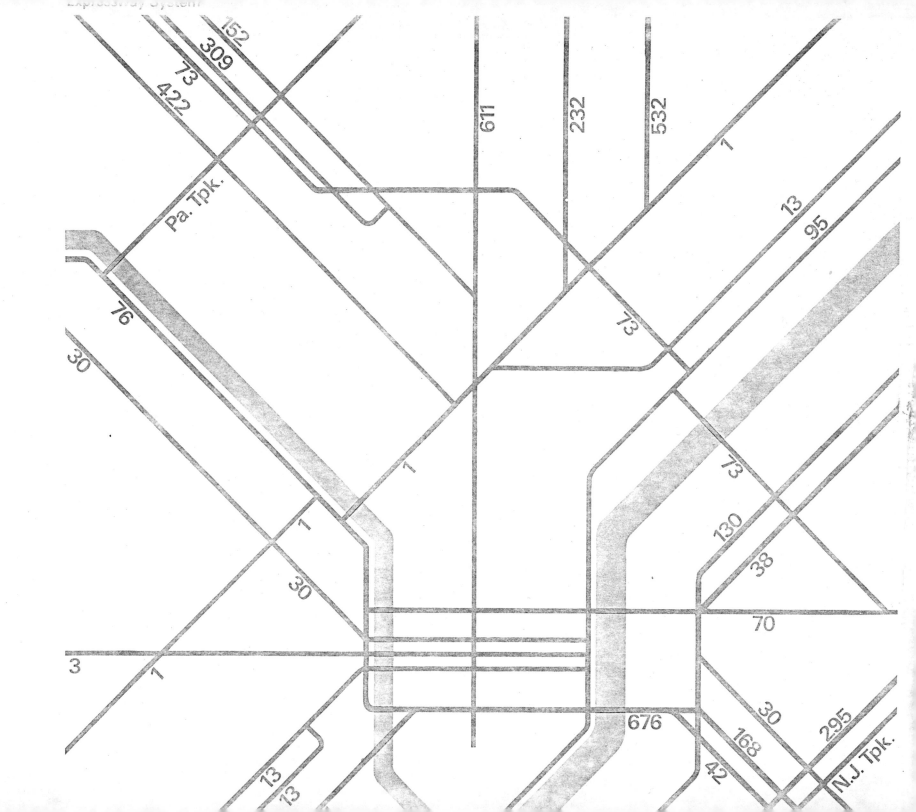

12-43

City and Regional Data

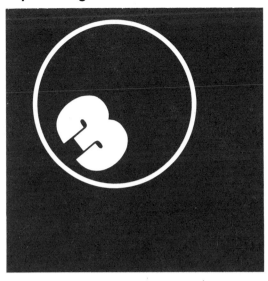

Plans and Planners

Man-Made Philadelphia

A Guide to Its Physical and Cultural Environment

Richard Saul Wurman
John Andrew Gallery

Photographs George Krause
and Howard Brunner
sponsored by
the Philadelphia chapter of
the A.I.A.

The routes and areas describe the city as it is today. But this present form is the result of development and change over a long period of time and is subject to a variety of influences. Population expansion and movement, street growth and urbanization, regional transportation—all influence the present form of the city. This form is, in turn, controlled through a series of legal and political districts that are designed to help it function and to provide the complex range of services required by the population.

Present form and patterns of growth are generally the result of a limited number of consciously developed public policies and plans. Many cities have simply grown without any controls, and the resultant form is dependent upon the network of streets. In all cases the final achievement is the result of work by individual architects who serve the needs of private clients and the public while working within the context of a broader image of the city.

The MIT Press
Cambridge, Massachusetts, and London, England

This book was implemented and produced by the Media/Design/Production Department of The MIT Press printed by Acme Printing Co. and bound by American Book-Stratford Press, Inc. in the United States of America

Library of Congress
catalog card number: 72-4534
ISBN 0 262 23058 5 (hardcover)
0 262 73031 6 (paperback)

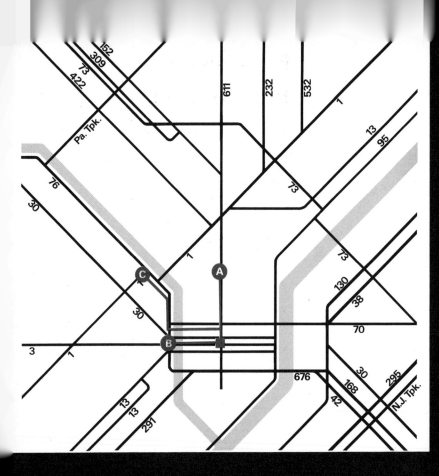

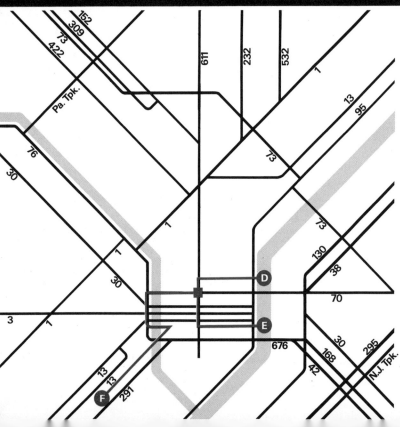

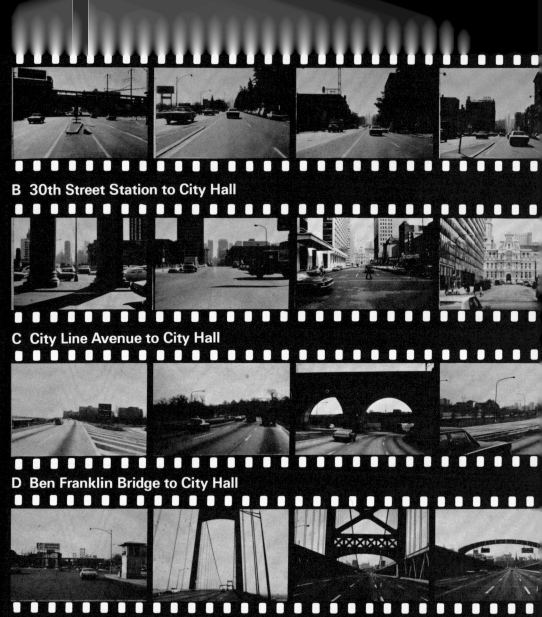

B 30th Street Station to City Hall

C City Line Avenue to City Hall

D Ben Franklin Bridge to City Hall

E Walt Whitman Bridge to City Hall

F Airport to City Hall

Routes
Public streets are the primary determinants of the form of the city. They range in scale from expressways to major arterial streets, and to smaller streets characteristic of a particular area of the city. Certain buildings stand out along the routes, either by position or architectural appearance, and usually serve as visual landmarks that help to identify specific places, or characteristics of specific areas. The routes, and the physical environment along them, are the initial and dominant experience of the city for all people.

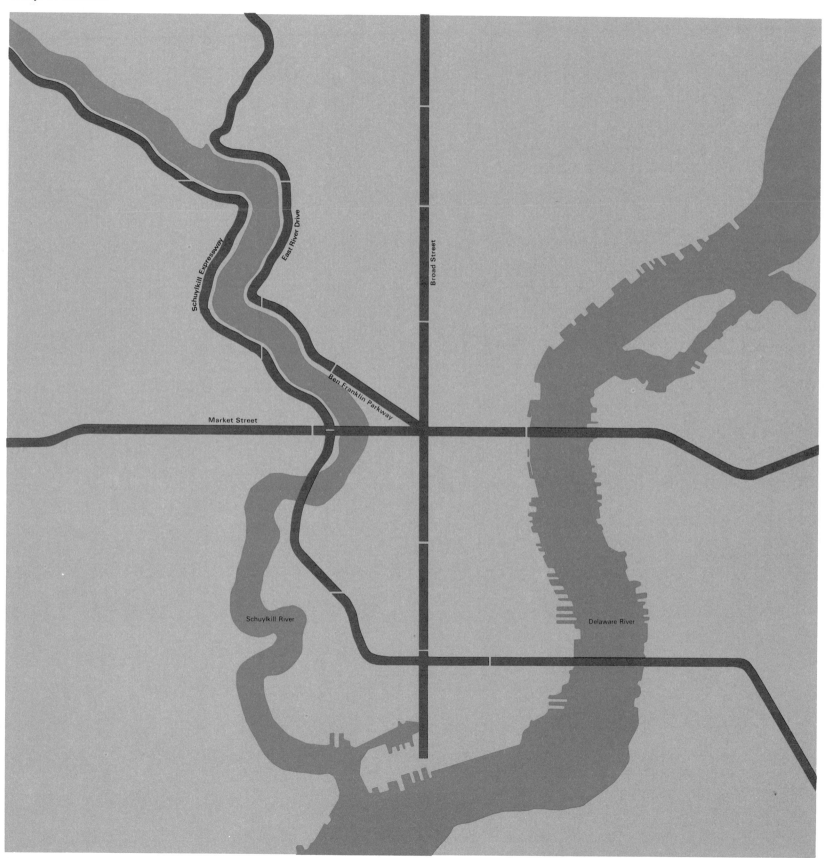

Market Street East

Market Street has been the main street of Philadelphia since William Penn's surveyor laid out the plan of the city in 1682. Originally called High Street, it was distinguished from other east-west streets by its width (100 feet as compared to 50 feet) and by its intersection with Broad Street in the Center Square. Commercial development began at the eastern end and gradually extended westward, taking advantage of the improved transportation Market Street's width provided. This transportation advantage was enhanced in the late nineteenth century with the completion of the Pennsylvania and Reading Railroad terminals and by the completion of the city's first subway system under Market Street in 1908.

Penn intended that no buildings be built between Front Street and the Delaware River, but inevitably warehouses and pier facilities began to proliferate around the expanding Port of Philadelphia. Many were cleared in 1850 when Delaware Avenue was created. Recently all structures in this area were demolished to make way for another road, the Delaware Expressway (Interstate 95), and the view, temporarily, is much as Penn intended. However, this view of the river is rapidly being transformed by the first-phase construction of Penn's Landing, a waterfront recreation and education center to be opened in 1975.

Many of the city's important institutions originated in the area between Front and Fourth streets. The first open-air markets were here and gave High Street its popular name, officially changed to Market Street in 1854. The first city hall was at the eastern end of the market in a structure similar to the Head House, still standing at Second and Pine. Christ Church, the first major church in the city, was constructed at Second Street just north of Market, even though at the time the principal residential areas were farther south. There are still a few examples of the commercial structures that once surrounded the markets, such as the group along North Front Street between Market and Arch streets, some recently restored buildings on Strawberry and Bank streets, and the Leland Building, a nineteenth-century example on South Third Street.

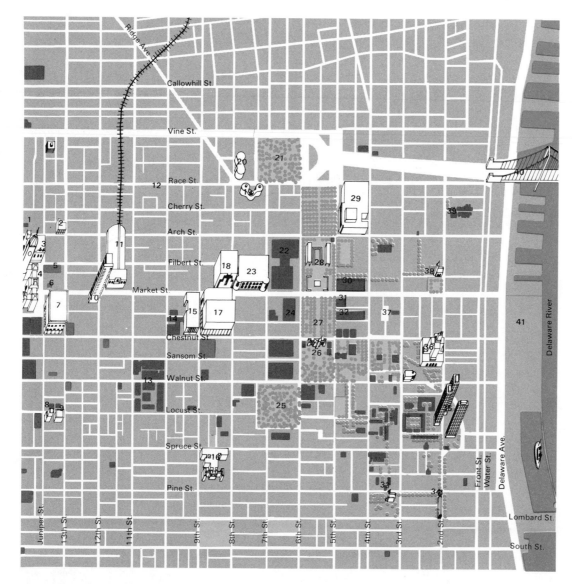
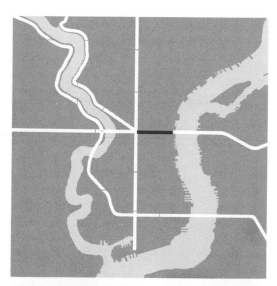

Wanamaker Eagle, 13th and Market

A similar mixture of eighteenth- and nineteenth-century residences and warehouses once existed between Fourth and Seventh streets. However, in the early 1940s many citizens became concerned about the deteriorating condition of Independence Hall and the area around it. Through their efforts, the Independence National Historical Park was created by Congress in 1948, and extensive restoration begun. Hundreds of buildings were demolished by the Commonwealth of Pennsylvania to create the three-block mall north of Independence Hall, and the adjacent blocks were subsequently cleared by the city for the new office development, Independence Mall.

From west of Seventh Street to City Hall, Market Street remains much as it was in the nineteenth century when it became the main shopping area of Philadelphia. The eastern end is distinguished by the rich collection of cast-iron-fronted buildings that comprise Lit Brothers Department Store and the western end by the John Wanamaker Store, noted for its large interior central court, which contains the largest pipe organ in the world and a 2,000 pound bronze eagle, both purchased from the St. Louis Exposition of 1904. The area in between is rich in variety and includes Chinatown two blocks north of Market at Tenth Street. Many of the buildings along the north side of Market Street, including the Reading Railroad Terminal with its open train shed, will be demolished as part of the city's urban renewal program. The Reading Terminal Market (entered from Twelfth Street) is the last surviving descendant of the old farm-

ers' markets. It contains goods as varied as the city's best ice cream (Bassetts), organic foods, and Amish baked goods and is a fascinating place to shop and browse.

The most architecturally significant building along this part of Market Street is the Philadelphia Savings Fund Society (PSFS) Building, the only major office building east of City Hall. Built during the Great Depression, it is remarkable for its excellent use of materials and unusual design. The banking room is located on the second floor, allowing the ground floor to be used for shopping. When completed in 1932, it was considered to be the most advanced skyscraper in the country. Even today, it is one of the outstanding buildings in the city and still the tallest after City Hall Tower.

Soft Pretzel
with Mustard

Reading Terminal

The Reading Railroad Terminal on Market Street opened in 1893. The terminal was built on land purchased from the Farmers Market, which had located there in the 1860s. As part of the sale the railroad agreed to provide a place for the market in its new terminal; the market reopened at its present location in late 1893.

The terminal was built to consolidate three passenger stations of the Reading, the principal ones being at Ninth and Green streets, and Broad and Callowhill streets. At the time of its construction the train shed was the largest singlespan shed in the country (266 feet).

PSFS Building, 12th and Market

Market Street near City Hall

Christ Church, 2nd and Market

Market Street West

Market Street West

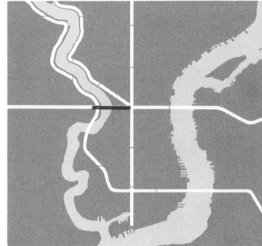

Penn Center at 16th

Penn's initial plan designated a Front Street at the western end of the city along the Schuylkill River, matching the Front Street along the Delaware. The streets were originally numbered in, toward the Center Square, and the present consecutive numbering system was not adopted until 1857. Penn hoped development would start along both riverfronts and move inward. However, there was no substantial growth along West Market Street until the late nineteenth century, following the construction of the Broad Street Station of the Pennsylvania Railroad (1881).

In recent years the area immediately west of City Hall was completely reconstructed. The Broad Street Station was demolished in 1953, along with the elevated tracks behind it referred to by Philadelphians as the "Chinese wall." In its place the Pennsylvania Railroad initiated construction of Penn Center, the first new commercial office project in the city since the completion of the PSFS Building twenty years earlier. Penn Center was recently extended by the city through the construction of an office building for its own use, the Municipal Services Building, and through the creation of several new public plazas around City Hall.

Although Penn Center extends as far west as Twentieth Street, its primary influence has been in the area of City Hall. Several additional buildings have been proposed or constructed adjacent to it among rapidly disappearing movie houses and pinball parlors. The mixture of marginal buildings, warehouses, and parking lots surrounding new office buildings increases west of Seventeenth Street. Office growth is continuing to expand westward, supported by the fine shopping areas along Chestnut Street one block to the south of Market Street and the new apartment buildings along John F. Kennedy Boulevard one block to the north. While the western edge of Penn's original town—along the Schuylkill River—will be preserved as a park from the Art Museum to South Street, office space will undoubtedly continue to expand across the river to connect with the Thirtieth Street Railroad Station.

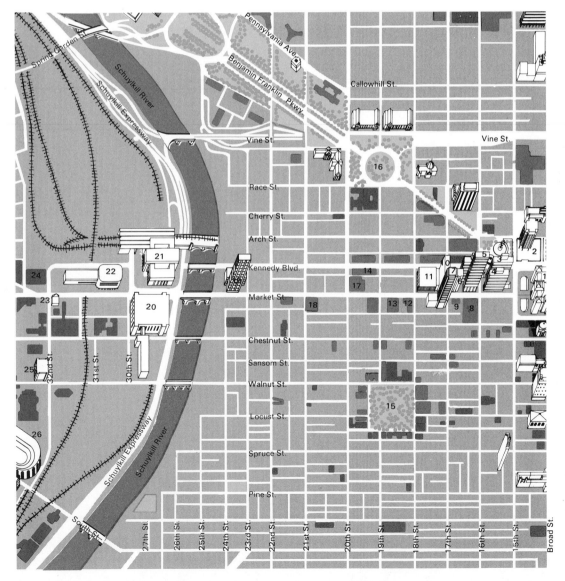

Market Street near 17th

ntil 1805 the Schuylkill River could be crossed ly by ferry or by a single bridge at Market reet. Roads radiated from the terminus of at bridge through West Philadelphia, with ly a few industries located along the west nk of the river. The completion of other idges and the increased accessibility provided the railroad subsequently attracted many gional institutions and activities to this lotion, such as the main post office.

Market Street continues beyond Thirtieth Street for another three miles to the city limit at Sixty-ninth Street. The University of Pennsylvania, Drexel University, the University City Science Center, and other institutions give way to residential areas such as Mill Creek and Haddington. Market Street itself changes considerably in character after Forty-sixth Street where the subway rises on elevated tracks in

the center of the street and overshadows the Fifty-second Street honky-tonk bars and the row houses with large porches and small front yards farther on.

ity Hall, Broad and Market

IVB Building, 17th and Market

Bulletin Building, 31st and Market

The Philadelphia Stock Exchange is the oldest in the country, having been founded in 1790, two years before New York's. Its first permanent home was in the Merchants Exchange Building designed by William Strickland in 1834. The Philadelphia Exchange merged with the Baltimore Exchange in 1949, the Washington, D.C. Exchange in 1953, and the Pittsburgh Exchange in 1969 and is now the largest stock exchange outside New York City.

3 Girard Plaza
15th near City Hall

Broad Street South

Broad Street South

Philadelphia clubs were started in response to the Blue Laws, to provide places to drink on Sundays and as the result of the fragmentation of social life caused by the city consolidation in 1854. The establishment men's clubs are the Philadelphia Club, Rittenhouse Club, Racquet Club, and the Union League. Many other clubs in the city originated for special purposes: the Locust Club (founded because some of the others refused to permit Jews to join); the Vespers New Year's Club, with over 5,000 members; the Acorn Club for women only; and the Franklin Inn Club for writers.

Broad Street was the other main street of Penn's plan. Like Market Street it was 100 feet in width, and the two streets intersected in the Center Square. Originally Broad Street was located at Twelfth Street but was moved to Fourteenth Street in the 1730s to accommodate the growth that was occurring predominantly in Philadelphia's eastern half. With the city-county consolidation in 1854, Broad Street became the city's longest street, extending twelve miles from the Delaware River to the city limits. It was the first street paved for automobiles (1894) and, like Market Street, became the location of a subway line initially opened in 1928, with additions made in 1936, 1956, and 1970.

South Broad Street had its major building boom in the late nineteenth and early twentieth centuries. The completion of City Hall encouraged the development of office and bank headquarters nearby, and now the area south of City Hall to Walnut Street is most representative of "establishment" Philadelphia. In the area are all of the major banks, as well as all of the major law offices and the prestigious Union League Club, the first Republican Club in the country and center of Philadelphia Republican life since 1865.

Immediately south of Walnut Street are many cultural and entertainment landmarks. Near the Bellevue-Stratford, the city's major hotel, is the Academy of Music, modeled after La Scala in Milan. The first movies in Philadelphia were shown in the Academy (1872), but it is better known for its outstanding acoustics and as the home of the Philadelphia Orchestra. Adjacent to it are the New Locust and Shubert theaters, and slightly east on Locust Street is a somewhat incompatible collection of honky-tonk bars and discotheques, which pass for Center City night life. The Young Men's and Women's Hebrew Association—one of the centers of avant garde art activity in the city—and the Philadelphia College of Art, which has begun to acquire nearby buildings for its expansion, complete the diversity of cultural offerings in the area.

Broad Street South
21 Anderson Playground
15 Atlantic Richfield Bldg.
9 Bellevue-Stratford
20 Children's Hospital of Phila.
1 City Hall
28 Columbus Playground
27 Federal Playground
8 Fidelity Bank
22 Frank Palumbo Rec. Center
2 Girard Bank
19 Hawthorne Square
18 Health Clinic (Public)
23 Italian Market
4 John Wanamaker Dept. Store
26 Norris Jr. High School
12 Phila. Academy of Music
16 Phila. College of Art
3 Phila. National Bank
5 Provident National Bank
24 Ridgeway Library
11 Rittenhouse Square
14 Shubert Theater
25 St. Rita R.C. Church
13 Sylvania Hotel
7 Union League Club
10 Washington Square
6 Western Savings Bank
17 YMHA

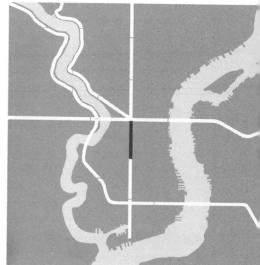

Girard Bank, Broad and Chestnut

South Street was the southern boundary of Penn's plan and is still the southern boundary of Center City Philadelphia. Along Broad Street the transition is immediately obvious. South Street consists of a number of small stores and craft shops mixed among totally deserted buildings left in the wake of a proposed crosstown expressway, now apparently abandoned. High-rise public housing buildings give an indication of the residential areas behind the chaotic assembly of gas stations and hamburger stands, which complete the Broad Street inventory in this area.

South Philadelphia was originally settled by the Swedes. Southwark, a small area east of Fifth Street, is the oldest section of the city. By the 1830s, South Philadelphia had become a black ghetto. Race riots occurred periodically until city consolidation in 1854, when the first municipal police force was established. In the early part of the twentieth century, South Philadelphia received most of the city's newly arriving immigrants. While many moved on to other sections of the city, the Italian population remained and today is the major influence there. South Broad Street reflects the religious orientation of the Italian community in the large and prominent Catholic churches interspersed with numerous funeral homes and typical Philadelphia row houses. The few major institutional buildings, such as the enormous Greek revival Ridgway Library, seem out of place. Originally built in 1876 for the Library Company of Philadelphia (first circulating library in the United States, founded in 1731), the building has been vacant since 1966 when the Library Company moved to its new quarters at Thirteenth and Locust streets.

Philadelphia College of Art, Broad and Pine

Drake Hotel,
1512 Spruce

The Philadelphia Orchestra was founded in 1900 and has performed continuously from that time in the Academy of Music. It has one of the largest collections of symphonic recordings of any orchestra in the world. The orchestra has had only four regular conductors throughout its 71-year history, the most famous being Leopold Stokowski (1912-1936) and Eugene Ormandy (1936 to the present).

The Academy of Music is the oldest opera house in continuous use in the United States. It was opened in 1857, the design and architect (Napoleon Le Brun) having been selected by a competition. At the time of its construction the central business area of the city was near Fifth and Sixth streets. Broad Street was selected as the site because it was a residential street, a quiet location free from vehicular noise. While most of the academy is modeled after La Scala in Milan, the grand ballroom is modeled after the Hall of Mirrors at Versailles. It was restored in 1962 for the enjoyment of the approximately 600,000 people who attend the academy's performances each year.

Bellevue-Stratford Hotel, Broad and Walnut

Union League, Broad and Sansom

Philadelphia Academy of Music, Broad and Locust

The first New Year's Day Mummer's Parade was held in 1876, but the parade did not receive official status until 1901 when forty-two groups were granted permits to march on Broad Street for monetary prizes awarded by the City Council. The "mummers" tradition comes from England, where groups of fantastically dressed pantomime troupes would parade through the streets at Christmas time. Brought to the colonies, this tradition merged with similar Swedish traditions in South Philadelphia, where the first mummers groups were formed. The original march was to Independence Hall, where pistols were fired, resulting in the name New Year's Shooters. Now the parade goes up Broad Street to City Hall and is attended by more than 400,000 people, while millions more watch on television.

Broad Street South

17 Barry Playground
10 Cemetery
5 Edward Bok Vocational School
13 Fell Public School
8 Guerin Rec. Center
16 Marconi Plaza
12 Methodist Hospital
15 Mollbore Terrace
1 Moyamensing Prison
11 Playground
6 South Phila. High School
4 Southwark Public School
3 St. Agnes Hospital
14 Stella Maria R.C. Church
9 Stephen Girard Public School
7 St. Luke's Church Rectory
2 St. Thomas Aquinas High School
18 U.S. Army Supply Depot

The Philadelphia Veterans Stadium is the largest stadium built in the U.S. in the past 25 years. It has a capacity of 65,000 for football and 47,145 for baseball. After 15 years of planning and several rejected sites and rejected designs, the stadium finally opened for the 1971 season. It is the home of the Philadelphia Phillies of the National Baseball League and the Philadelphia Eagles of the National Football League.

The real South Philadelphia institutions are within the residential neighborhoods east of Broad Street. The outdoor Italian Market along Ninth Street, between Catherine Street and Washington Avenue, is a mecca for food shoppers from all over the city, as well as for browsing visitors. Adjacent to it are some of the city's best Italian restaurants and the only real night club (Palumbo's). The nearby Fleisher Art School provides free art education; the Settlement Music School provides free musical education for children and was the starting place for the careers of a number of prominent Philadelphia-born musicians, such as Mario Lanza and Marion Anderson. One of the most famous "institutions" associated with Broad Street and South Philadelphia is the Philadelphia String Band and the Mummers' Parade of New Year's Day, which originates at Broad and Snyder streets.

Broad Street terminates with a large sports complex and the U.S. Naval Base. John F. Kennedy Stadium was originally built for the U.S. Sesquicentennial Exposition (1926) and is seldom used except for the annual Army-Navy football game. Nearby are the Spectrum Indoor Arena and the city's new football and baseball stadium (Veterans Stadium). Franklin D. Roosevelt Park, the site of the Sesquicentennial Celebration, supplements these with informal recreation facilities. Within the park are the American-Swedish Historical Museum, with exhibits showing the lives of these earliest settlers and their continuing contributions to the city, and Belair, a Flemish-style, early eighteenth-century house that is one of the oldest buildings in the city.

The U.S. Navy was founded in Philadelphia, and many of the major ships of the Revolution were constructed here. The Naval Base was begun in 1801 and located at South Broad Street in 1876. Over 150 vessels, including several battleships, are stored in the mothball fleet. The base in completely open only once a year on Armed Forces Day in May. During the rest of the year guided bus tours are available, but the best view is from the excursion boat that travels south along the Delaware River from its pier adjacent to the Olympia, Admiral Dewey's flagship at the battle of Manila Bay ("You may fire when you are ready, Gridley!"). The pier is located beneath the Benjamin Franklin Bridge at Race Street and Delaware Avenue. An 88-year-old square rigger, the Gazela Primeiro, is permanently docked at the foot of Vine Street. It was given to the Philadelphia Maritime Museum after having crossed the Atlantic by the same route as that taken by Columbus in 1492.

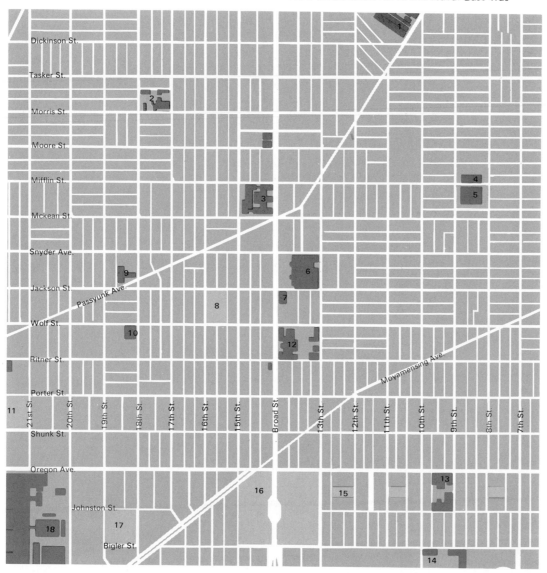

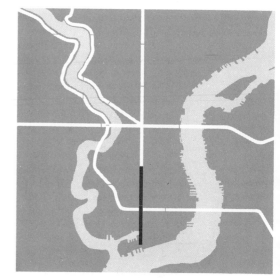

Italian Market, 9th and Christian

Sports Complex: Veterans Stadium, Spectrum, and J.F.K. Stadium, Broad and Paterson

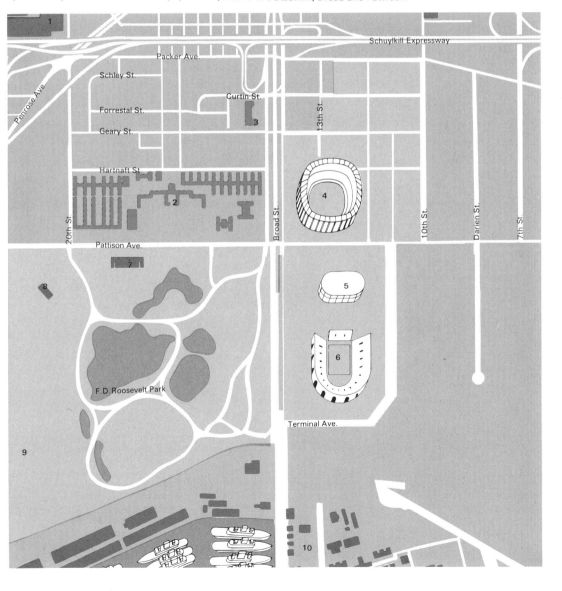

Mifflin Square, 6th and Ritner Street

Navy Yard, End of South Broad

Navy Yard, Crane

The Philadelphia Naval Base and Shipyard were founded in 1801 and located on League Island in 1876. The base now covers 1,600 acres and is the headquarters of the Fourth Naval District. It contains over 150 mothballed ships, the largest over-head crane in the world, and a 1,400-bed hospital nearby.

Broad Street South
7 American-Swedish Museum
3 Aquarama Bldg.
8 Belair House
9 Golf Course
6 J.F. Kennedy Stadium
5 Spectrum Indoor Sports Arena
1 U.S. Army Supply Depot
10 U.S. Naval Base
2 U.S. Naval Hospital
4 Veterans Stadium

The first naval academy was started in Philadelphia in 1839. It was located in the Naval Asylum, still standing at Twenty-fourth St. and Grays Ferry Avenue, until 1845 when the academy was moved to Annapolis.

The Port of Philadelphia is the largest freshwater port in the world and the second largest import port in the U.S., handling over 54 million tons annually. It is part of a series of ports that stretch 50 miles along the Delaware River from Wilmington, Del. to Trenton, N.J. Collectively they are known as Ameriport. From 1954 to 1964 the Army Corps of Engineers increased the main channel to a depth of 40 feet and a width of 400 feet along a length of 32 miles. Now, more than 5,500 cargo ships per year call at the port, with freight service to 75 countries.

Broad Street North

In colonial times the area north of Center City Philadelphia was known as the Northern Liberties. Ridge Avenue was its major street, connecting the area to Germantown and the northwest. Broad Street was just another residential street that began to develop after 1870. However, with the completion of the subway in 1928, Broad Street became the main axis for growth. Consequently, major commercial and institutional development is relatively recent and widely dispersed.

Immediately north of City Hall are the Municipal Services Building and Masonic Temple. Masonic Temple is open to the public for scheduled tours through a variety of rooms decorated in exotic architectural styles. Oriental Hall and the cathedral-like Renaissance Hall are particularly impressive. North of Arch Street, Center City peters out into commercial and industrial shops, providing wholesale services to the main business area. The Pennsylvania Academy of the Fine Arts, an architectural masterpiece designed by Frank Furness, is often overlooked among its nondescript neighbors. The academy is the oldest art school in the country and has a permanent collection of American art from colonial times to the present.

Vine Street was the northern boundary of Penn's original city. A depressed expressway along its present route will shortly require the demolition of Louis I. Kahn's AF of L Medical Building east of Broad Street. Today, however, the real point of transition to North Philadelphia is Spring Garden Street. The State Office Building on the southwest corner and the Philadelphia Inquirer Building are the last major office buildings.

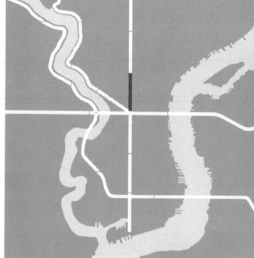

Municipal Services Building, Broad and J.F.K. Boulevard

Immediately to the north of Spring Garden Street, Malcolm X High School marks the transition to a physically and socially distinct area. North Philadelphia is now the city's major black ghetto. The area is rather uniformly developed with row houses of two and three stories built during the nineteenth century. Philadelphia is noted for its quantity of single-family houses, and North Philadelphia's are representative of the general pattern and scale. This residential area actually begins north of Girard Avenue, where a series of older mansions, including the elegant Widener Mansion, remain intact in an area of general physical decay.

Philadelphia Life Insurance Company, Broad near Arch

AF of L/CIO Medical Center, 13th and Vine

Masonic Temple, Broad and J.F.K. Boulevard

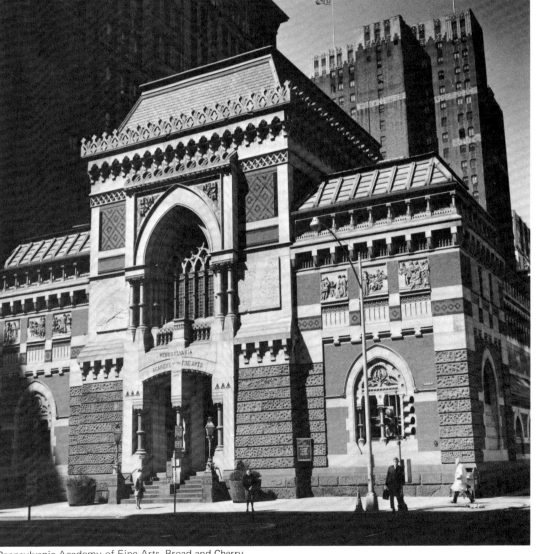

Pennsylvania Academy of Fine Arts, Broad and Cherry

The Pennsylvania Academy of Fine Arts was founded in 1809. It succeeded the Columbianum or American Academy of Fine Arts founded in 1794 by Charles Wilson Peale and thirty other artists. In 1807 the property of the academy was divided into shares of stock. (There are now 3,500 shares held by 655 shareholders.) By 1810 the academy was well on the way to establishing a school and in 1811 held its first annual exhibition. Among the exhibitors in these early years were Thomas Sully, John Singleton Copley, Gilbert Stuart, and Charles Wilson Peale. The academy's first building was at Tenth and Chestnut streets. This was partially destroyed by fire in 1845 and reconstructed by John Haviland. Its present building, designed by Frank Furness, was opened in 1876 and should be visited. Among the academy's notable paintings are Thomas Eakins's portrait of Walt Whitman, Sully's portrait of George Frederick Cooke as Richard III, and Benjamin West's Death on a Pale Horse.

Very few institutions were located here in the early years. A few churches are notable, but the Eastern State Penitentiary and Girard College are the only major historic institutions. Girard College was built on the farm of self-made financier Stephen Girard, who specified in his will that the school educate white male orphans. In 1968 the Supreme Court required the college to open to black male students as well as white. A fifteen-foot wall—also specified by Girard—still surrounds the school, and the enormous Greek revival Founders Hall marks his memory.

Most of the major changes in North Philadelphia are the result of twentieth-century urban renewal. The first urban renewal project in the country was started in the Yorktown area east of Broad Street in 1947. Almost every structure was demolished in the twenty-five-block area from Girard Avenue north to Columbia Avenue, and new row houses were constructed, providing the first opportunity for middle-income blacks to remain in North Philadelphia. The area east of Yorktown to Fifth Street was also cleared, and a number of residential communities were begun around a newly built Ukranian cathedral with a prominent mosaic gold dome. Recent residential improvement projects in the area have been on a scattered basis and have tried to restore, rather than demolish, existing dwellings. Though many vacant houses have been bought by the city and reconstructed, many thousands still remain unoccupied.

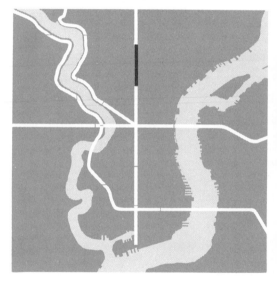

Widener Mansion, Broad and Girard

One of the major influences on North Philadelphia has been the growth of Temple University, north of Yorktown. Founded in 1884, Temple is now a state university with over 40,000 students. The main academic campus has grown rapidly, and new dormitories, classroom buildings, libraries, and a gymnasium have recently been completed. Columbia Avenue, along Temple's southern border, is the main commercial street of the black community in North Philadelphia. Adjacent to it are important cultural institutions such as the Heritage House, the Church of the Advocate, and the R.W. Brown Boys' Club. Progress Plaza, south of Temple, is a black-owned shopping center organized by the Reverend Leon Sullivan, founder of the Opportunities Industrialization Center (OIC). The Hartranft Community, north of Temple University, is the location of one of the city's most innovative school buildings and community-based redevelopment efforts.

The densely populated North Philadelphia area terminates at the North Philadelphia Station of the Penn Central. Beyond it row houses are set back from Broad Street, and there is a greater feeling of spaciousness. Temple University's Medical Center, just north of the station, and the Albert Einstein Medical Center (Northern Division) are the only major institutions in an area that becomes increasingly more suburban. The Olney Avenue shopping area is almost a satellite center in its own right, so remote is it from downtown Philadelphia.

Paley Library, Temple University, 13th and Berks

Columbia Avenue near 15th

North Broad Street Station, Broad and Allegeheny

Row Houses, North Philadelphia

Graffiti

Temple University was started in 1884 and became a state institution in 1966. The university has twenty-four schools and colleges, including Temple Hospital and Medical School (now the Health Sciences Center); Tyler School of Art in Elkins Park; and the two-year liberal arts and horticulture school on the Ambler Campus, also the location of the University's Summer Music Festival.

Benjamin Franklin Parkway

Benjamin Franklin Parkway

The construction of the Benjamin Franklin Parkway in the early twentieth century was the only significant modification of the grid plan of William Penn. The parkway was originally proposed in 1892 and consisted, even in the initial plans, of a baroque boulevard intended to create a diagonal vista that would break the monotony of the grid plan. After many delays the parkway concept was taken up in 1910 by the Fairmount Park Art Association, which engaged French landscape designer Jacques Greber to create the final plan. Greber's plan produced the desired uninterrupted vista from Faire Mount (as the slight hill at the western end was historically known), where a new art museum was to be erected, to the City Hall Tower.

Following Greber's plan, a new design for the Art Museum was approved and construction begun on the east and west wings while fund-raising went on for the center portion. Some parts of the building have still not been completed. Construction of the Parkway itself began in 1917 and proceeded from west to east. The western end was modeled after the Champs Elysees with wide roads, many rows of trees, and substantial setbacks for the buildings. Few of the suggested buildings were ever completed, with two notable exceptions, the Philadelphia Museum of Art and the modest Rodin Museum and Courtyard, a substitute for a more grandiose proposal. The plaza and fountains in front of the Art Museum were begun, but redesigned and completed in 1967. The present appearance of this part of the Parkway is dominated by several recent apartment buildings.

The central section of the Parkway required the complete redesign of Logan Circle and is described in Section 2. The eastern section is intentionally more urban, and the narrow spatial connection to City Hall, proposed by Greber, has been accomplished in recent years by the addition of several new apartment buildings, the United Fund Office Building, the Friends Select School, and the Pennwalt Office Building. Originally, the Parkway terminated at City Hall. This arrangement changed in the 1950s coincident with the development of Penn Center. The last block was closed to traffic, and John F. Kennedy Plaza on top of an underground parking garage became the new terminus. A national competition was held for the design of a fountain for this plaza, but the winning proposal was never built, and the present pool and spray were substituted in its place.

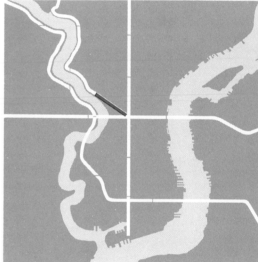

Among the more interesting aspects of the Parkway are the design controls that were established and adopted by special ordinance of the city council. These controls apply to all buildings within 200 feet of the Parkway and set specific height limitations and setback requirements for different sections. They are in force, even to this day, under the jurisdiction of the city's art commission.

Ben Franklin Parkway
Phases of Construction

United Fund Building, 18th and Ben Franklin Parkway

The Philadelphia Museum of Art, End of Ben Franklin Parkway

Rodin Museum, 22nd and Ben Franklin Parkway

Logan Circle, 19th and Ben Franklin Parkway

Parkway House
Apartments

Schuylkill Expressway

Schuylkill Expressway North

The major regional automobile access to Philadelphia is via the Schuylkill Expressway (Interstate 76). Completed in 1955, it is the only expressway serving Center City and is, therefore, heavily used and often congested or at a standstill. Because it was built through many developed areas, its design standards are far below present highway requirements, and it has consequently been nicknamed the "Sure Kill Crawlway."

The northern portion of the expressway is supplemented by East and West River drives in Fairmount Park. The section from Market Street to Girard Avenue presents two substantially different views. On the west the view is dominated by the 120 acres of railroad tracks north of the Thirtieth Street Station. To the east is one of the most striking views of Philadelphia. Across the river in East Park, the templelike Art Museum on the hill towers above both the delicate Boat House Row and the old city waterworks, with City Hall Tower and the PSFS Building dominating the skyline beyond.

North of Girard Avenue the expressway travels through Fairmount Park. The view to east and west is of heavily treed slopes with an occasional glimpse of a park mansion roof or the prominently illuminated dome of Memorial Hall appearing above the trees. At Strawberry Mansion Bridge there is a public boathouse opposite the entrance to the Laurel Hill Cemetery in the East Park.

At the City Line Interchange the expressway leaves the city, although the view across the river is of Philadelphia. The East Falls high-rise public housing is situated prominently on the east bank, and farther on, the steep slopes of Manayunk and Roxborough are covered with modest houses and churches in a manner reminiscent of European hill towns. City Line Avenue itself is a substantial commercial street just south of the expressway. The Presidential Apartments and Holiday Motor Inn can be seen on the skyline from the expressway. Several Philadelphia television stations are located in the same area. On the Montgomery County side of City Line are fine stores, such as Lord and Taylor and Saks Fifth Avenue. The Schuylkill Expressway connects with the Pennsylvania Turnpike at Valley Forge, six miles from the City Line Interchange.

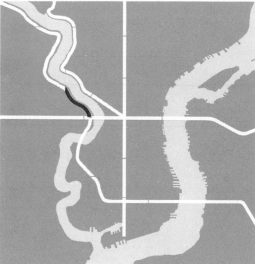

Post Office and 30th Street Station, 30th and Market

Expressway View North

Night View of Center City from Expressway

There are 79,500 street-lights and 15,850 alley lights in Philadelphia. Each year about 17,000 streetlights are replaced at a cost of $160,000.

Spring Garden Street Bridge and Philadelphia Electric Tower

Philadelphia Electric Company Tower at Night

Schuylkill Expressway South

Along the southern portion of the expressway, from Market Street to the Grays Ferry Avenue Bridge, the view to the east is of the Center City skyline. To the west is the Philadelphia Civic Center and Franklin Field with the new high-rise dormitories towering above the other buildings on the University of Pennsylvania campus. South of Grays Ferry Avenue the physical and olfactory environment changes. Small South Philadelphia row houses or marginal commercial buildings on one side of the expressway face an exotic miniature city of pastel-colored storage tanks, refinery pipes, and gas-flaming towers. The expressway leads westward to the Philadelphia Airport along a route lined with storage tanks. An automobile crusher completes this surrealistic landscape. The main part of the expressway continues east past the South Broad Street sports complex to the Walt Whitman Bridge leading to New Jersey.

Oil Refineries along the Schuylkill Expressway

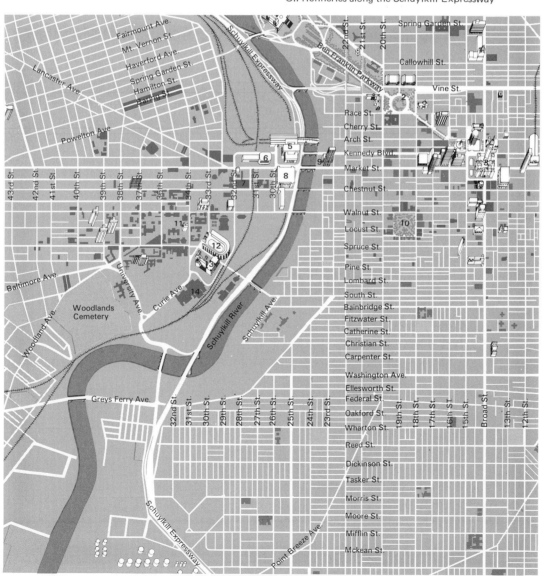

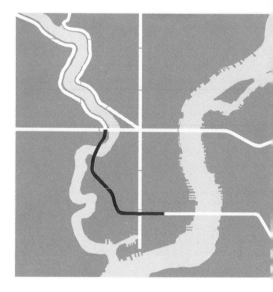

Tank Farm along Schuylkill Expressway

Penrose Avenue Bridge, South Philadelphia

Automobile Crusher, Penrose Avenue

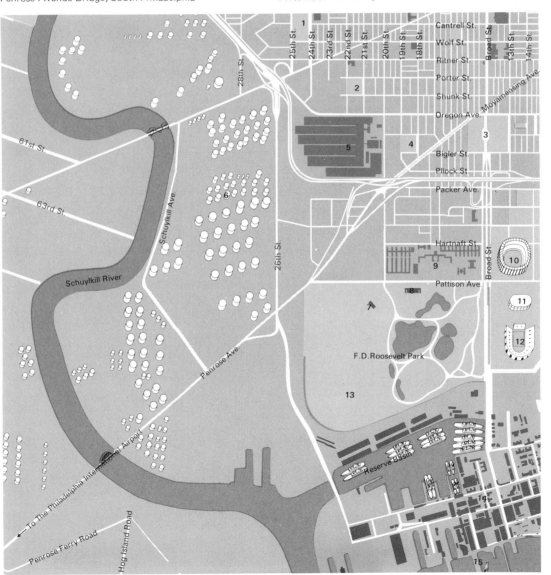

Schuylkill Expressway South

8 American-Swedish Museum
6 Atlantic Refining Company
7 Belair House
2 Girard Park
13 Golf Course
12 J.F.K. Stadium
3 Marconi Plaza
4 Playground
11 Spectrum Sports Arena
5 U.S. Army Supply Depot
14 U.S. Naval Base
9 U.S. Naval Hospital
10 Veterans Stadium
1 Wilson Park
15 World's Largest Crane

Each year the city tows away approximately 26,000 abandoned cars, or about one every twenty minutes.

The Walt Whitman Bridge was opened in 1957 and named for the great American poet who died in Camden, New Jersey. It is 6.5 miles in overall length, with a main span of 2,000 feet, and carries over 31 million cars per year.

Areas

Housing, commerce, and industry all expand along movement systems. These areas invariably touch on the major routes of the city and then grow out from them into fairly well defined areas of consistent use. Within most cities there are a limited number of areas of particular interest—downtown, universities, primary residential areas—each with its own architectural environment.

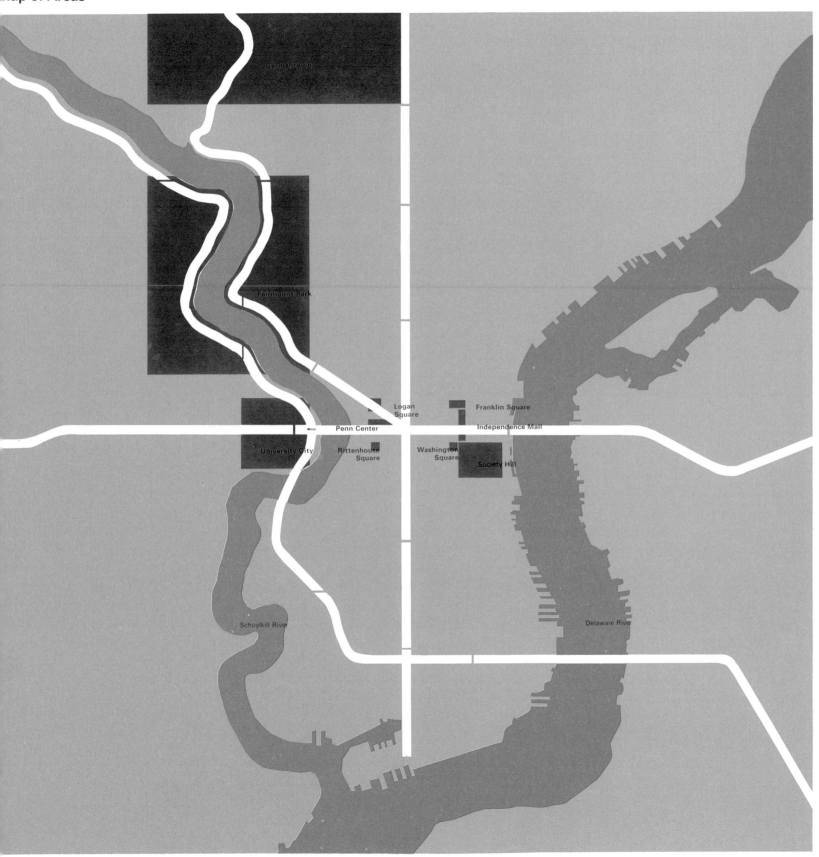

Germantown

Fairmount Park

Logan
Square

Franklin Square

Penn Center

Independence Mall

University City

Rittenhouse
Square

Washington
Square

Society Hill

Schuylkill River

Delaware River

Penn Center

In Penn's plan the Center Square was set aside for future public buildings. The site was used for a variety of purposes, including the first city waterworks in the country (1801). The present city hall was finally located there after a public referendum in 1870 asking citizens to choose between Center Square and Washington Square. (The vote was 51,263 to 32,825.) Modeled after the Louvre in Paris, it was finally completed in 1901 after twenty-nine years of construction and is one of the largest municipal buildings in the world. Alexander Calder (grandfather of the contemporary sculptor) designed the tower and the many pieces of sculpture that adorn the building, including the 37-foot-high statue of William Penn on top of the tower. There is an unwritten law in the city that no building shall be taller than the tower, and consequently the view from its observation deck, open free to the public, is unmatched.

With the completion of City Hall, the surrounding area became the center for government and finance. In the 1920s, plans were put forward for the demolition of the Pennsylvania Railroad's Broad Street Station to the west and the construction of a new station at Thirtieth Street. Thirtieth Street Station was built, but the rest of the project was delayed by the Depression and World War II until 1953, when the Broad Street Station and "Chinese wall" of elevated tracks behind it were finally demolished.

The original plans for the new Penn Center, developed by the City Planning Commission, organized office buildings around a lower-level pedestrian area, open to the sky. Unfortunately, the final plans were modified substantially for real estate and financial considerations. Fragments of the original ideas were retained, resulting in a usually barren pedestrian esplanade and an unattractive lower-level shopping area, both of which are seldom used.

Part of the project included the creation of a new street along the northern edge of the site. John F. Kennedy Boulevard and all of the buildings along it, with the exception of the Suburban Station, have been built since 1958 and were consciously designed to produce a "canyon" appearance similar to New York City streets.

The final office building in Penn Center was completed in 1970. Earlier, the city had extended the project by adding the Municipal Services Building and Plaza for its own use and to the west of these a public parking garage, which is topped by the John F. Kennedy Plaza. Another plaza to the west of City Hall and several other office buildings surrounding it are under construction.

One of the most interesting features of Penn Center is the underground concourse system. This was the first consciously designed lower-level walkway in a major city and has been the precedent for subsequent programs in Montreal, Fort Worth, and San Francisco, all of which have been carried out with greater imagination and quality. The concourse was designed to connect major transportation terminals (bus, railroad, and subway) and was originally intended to be fully open to natural light. Only a few courtyards were actually built; the one at Fifteenth Street, which is integrated into the subway station, is the most successful. The concourse area connects this subway station to the Surburban Railroad Station, bus terminal, the underground parking garage, and the public areas of several office buildings designed to extend the concourse-courtyard effect. It is part of a larger system projected by the city, which will ultimately extend from Eighth Street to Seventeenth Street and connect all transportation terminals along an enclosed mall lined with stores and entrances to new office buildings.

Head of Statue of William Penn

The statue of William Penn, atop City Hall, designed by Alexander Milne Calder, is the largest sculpture on a building in the world. Weighing 53,523 pounds, the 37-foot-high statue was brought to the City Hall courtyard in 1893 where it was displayed until 1894 before being moved to the top of the tower. The statue faces northeast toward Penn Treaty Park, the site where Penn reportedly concluded his negotiations with the Indians.

The city owns three major office buildings for its 35,000 administrative employees.

Penn Center Esplanade

Skating Rink, 17th and Market.

IBM Building, 17th and Market

Central Penn Bank, 16th and Market

Penn Center Above Ground

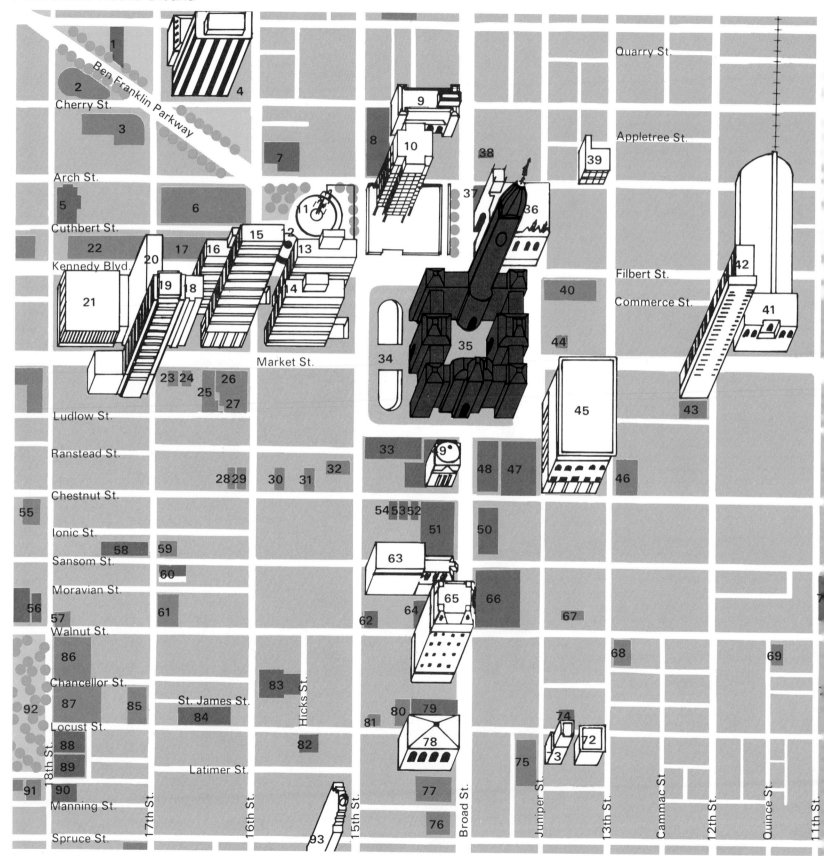

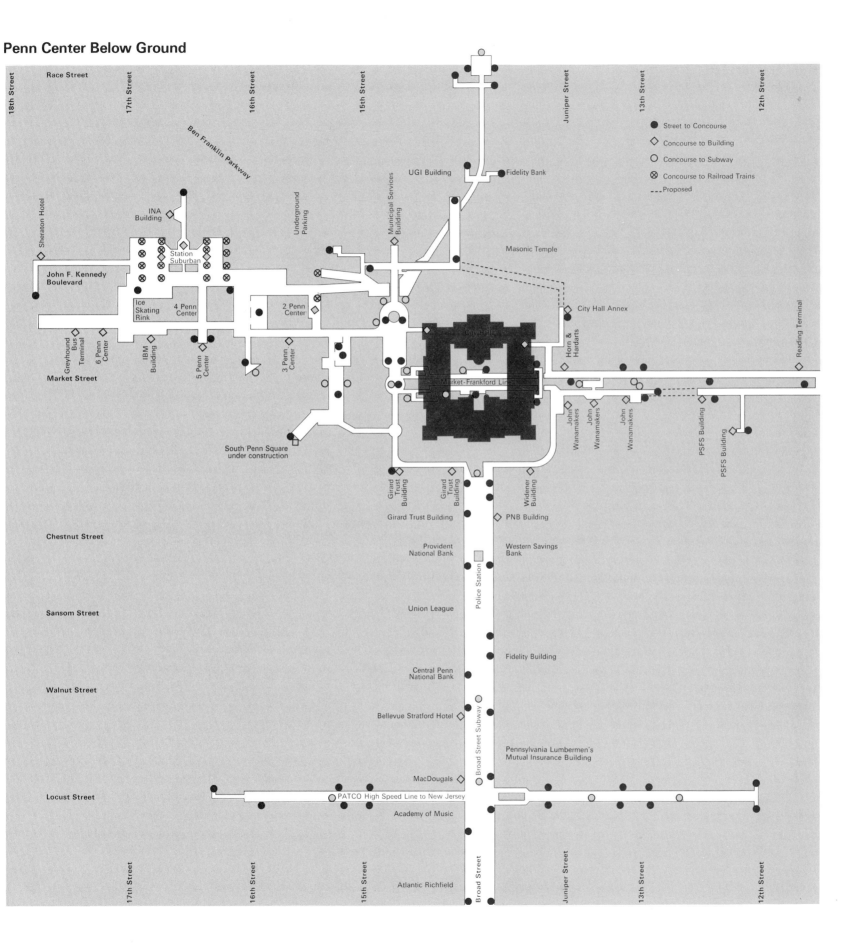

Race Street

Ben Franklin Parkway

18th Street
17th Street
16th Street
15th Street
Juniper Street
13th Street
12th Street

● Street to Concourse
◇ Concourse to Building
○ Concourse to Subway
⊗ Concourse to Railroad Trains
--- Proposed

UGI Building
Fidelity Bank

Sheraton Hotel

INA Building

Station Suburban

John F. Kennedy Boulevard

Municipal Services Building

Masonic Temple

Ice Skating Rink
4 Penn Center
2 Penn Center
City Hall Annex

City Hall

Underground Parking

Reading Terminal

Greyhound Bus Terminal
6 Penn Center
IBM Building
5 Penn Center
3 Penn Center

Market Street

Horn & Hardarts
Market-Frankford Line

John Wanamakers
John Wanamakers
John Wanamakers

PSFS Building
PSFS Building

South Penn Square under construction

Girard Trust Building
Girard Trust Building
Widener Building

Girard Trust Building
PNB Building

Chestnut Street

Provident National Bank
Western Savings Bank

Police Station

Sansom Street

Union League

Fidelity Building

Central Penn National Bank

Walnut Street

Bellevue Stratford Hotel

Broad Street Subway

Pennsylvania Lumbermen's Mutual Insurance Building

Locust Street

MacDougals

PATCO High Speed Line to New Jersey

Academy of Music

17th Street
16th Street
15th Street
Broad Street
Juniper Street
13th Street
12th Street

Atlantic Richfield

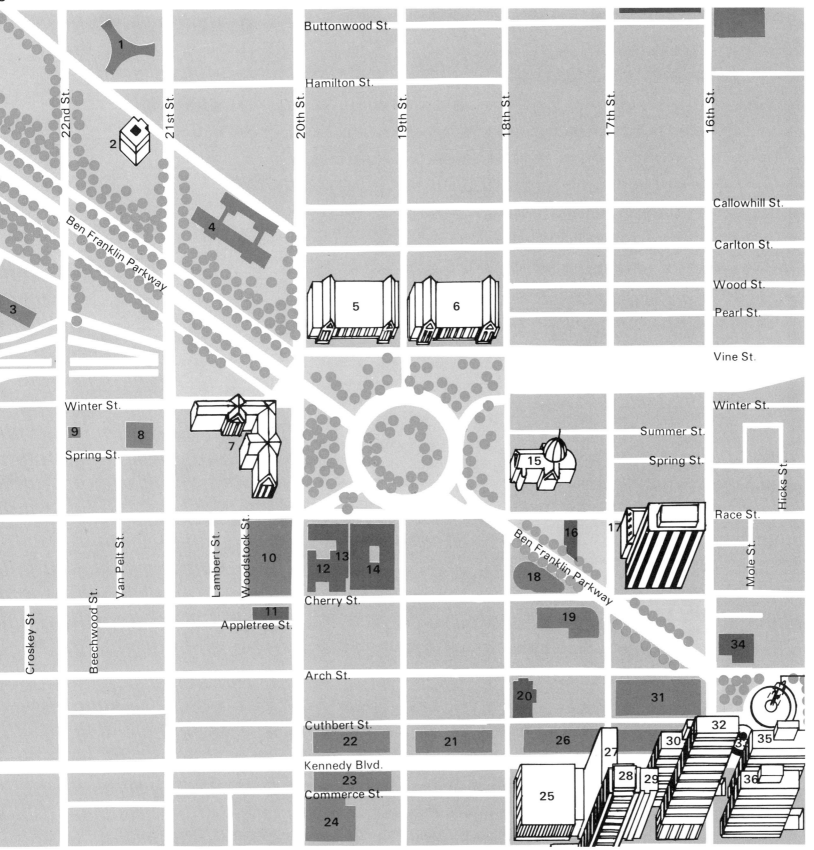

Logan Circle

Of the four original squares designated for common use in the Penn plan, Logan Circle has had the most varied history. In the eighteenth century it was first used for burial grounds and then converted to pastures and a site for public executions. It was rebuilt in 1825 and named after James Logan, a secretary to Penn and Chief Justice of Pennsylvania, who established the largest private library in the colonies, preserved intact by the Library Company of Philadelphia.

The present circular form of the square resulted from the construction of the Benjamin Franklin Parkway. At that time two of the major buildings were already in their present locations: the Cathedral of Saints Peter and Paul, and the Academy of Natural Sciences, which was established during the Centennial Celebration in 1876. Greber and Paul Gret added the Free Library and the Court Building to the north, clearly

modeled on the buildings of the Place de la Concorde in Paris, and the Franklin Institute on the west. The institute houses an extensive science museum and library, as well as the Fels Planetarium and Astronomical Observatory, all of which are open to the public. In recent years the area to the southwest has been greatly improved. The Moore College of Art—the oldest art school for girls in the United States—was added at the southwest corner in 1960, and the small residential areas behind it were gradually rehabilitated through the efforts of individual homeowners.

The Academy of Natural Sciences was founded in 1812 at Second and Market streets and moved to its present location in 1876. Its collection includes 150,000 bird specimens; 2,000,000 insects; 13,000,000 shells, one of the finest collections in the world; and an outstanding research library of 150,000 volumes.

Franklin Institute, 20th and Ben Franklin Parkway

Cathedral of Saints Peter and Paul, Logan Circle

Logan Circle, 19th and Ben Franklin Parkway

Rittenhouse Square

Of all the original squares, Rittenhouse Square is probably the best known outside Philadelphia. It has always been of great concern to the public and was the only one of the four squares not used as a burial ground. In the nineteenth century it was named in honor of David Rittenhouse, an outstanding colonial scientist and astronomer, and public funds were collected for the improvement of the square and the erection of a fountain.

The area surrounding the square became the outstanding residential section of the city in the nineteenth century. The brownstones along Spruce Street, Locust Street, and the 1800 block of Delancey Place are good examples of some of the fine row houses that still determine the character of the neighborhood. Most of the mansions that used to surround the square have been razed, but a few remain and are used by specialized institutions such as the Penn Athletic Club and Rittenhouse Club on the north, the Curtis Institute and Art Alliance at the southwest corner, and the Rosenback Museum of rare manuscripts and antique furniture on nearby Delancey Place. Several interesting early twentieth-century apartment buildings remain along the south side of the square, but these are gradually being outnumbered by contemporary apartment buildings.

The present character of the square is a reflection more of the diversity of people who gather there than of the surrounding architecture. These include elegant Philadelphia ladies and distinguished visitors from the Barclay Hotel, nurses and maids, and an extensive assortment of folk singers and hippies, for whom the square is the chief meeting place. Among other events, the Spring Flower Show, June Clothesline Art Exhibit, the Dog Show, and the Easter Parade are all held here.

Trinity Church, Walnut and Rittenhouse Square

1800 Block, Delancey Place

Rittenhouse Square, 19th and Walnut

Clothesline Art Exhibit, Rittenhouse Square

Barclay Hotel, 18th and Rittenhouse Square

Penn Athletic Club, 18th and Walnut

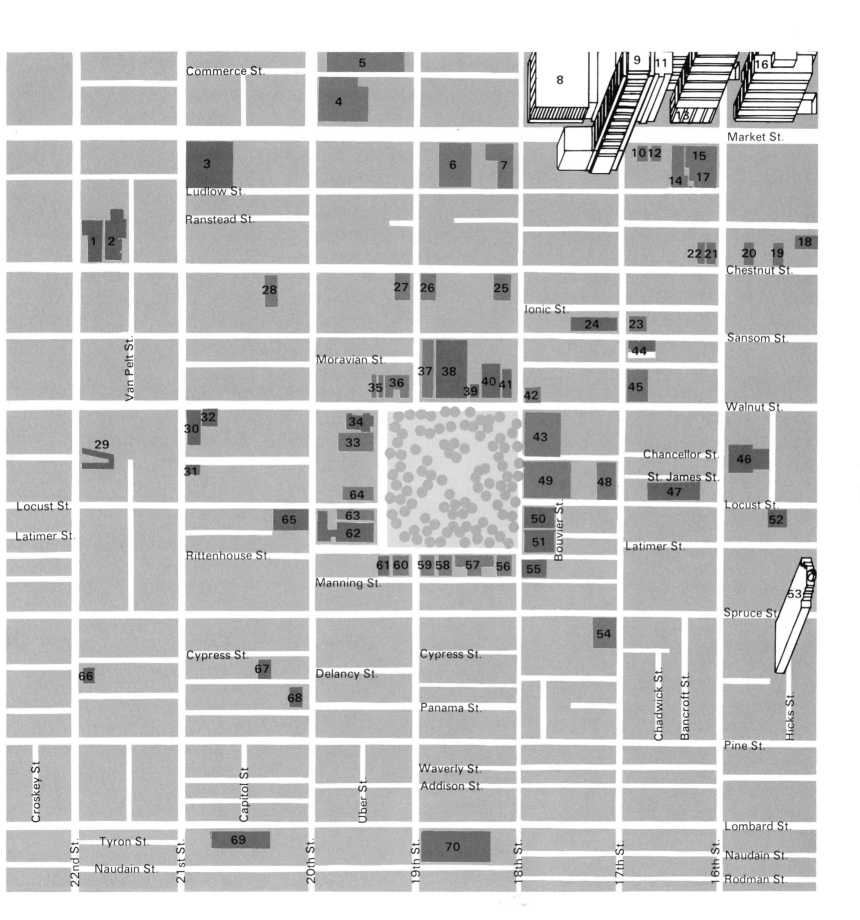

Commerce St.

Market St.

Ludlow St.

Ranstead St.

Van Pelt St.

Chestnut St.

Ionic St.

Sansom St.

Moravian St.

Walnut St.

Chancellor St.

St. James St.

Locust St.

Latimer St.

Bouvier St.

Rittenhouse St.

Manning St.

Latimer St.

Spruce St.

Cypress St.

Cypress St.

Delancy St.

Panama St.

Chadwick St.

Bancroft St.

Hicks St.

Pine St.

Waverly St.

Addison St.

Lombard St.

Tyron St.

Naudain St.

Naudain St.

Rodman St.

Croskey St

22nd St.

21st St.

Capitol St.

20th St.

Uber St.

19th St.

18th St.

17th St.

16th St.

Washington Square

Washington Square was used for a burial ground until 1825, when it was opened to the public and named after George Washington. In the early twentieth century, when much of the surrounding area was in disrepair, it achieved a colorful reputation that caused it to be closed for a time by the police. Today it is generally filled with the residents of adjacent apartment houses, and because it is the site of the Tomb of the Unknown Soldier of the Revolutionary War, it is often the focus for patriotic celebrations.

The row houses to the northwest on Walnut Street were the first built on a speculative basis in the city. They sold poorly because the square was considered too far west for residential development, even in 1800. Consequently, the neighborhood became mainly institutional and commercial. On the east side of the square the Atheneum, a private library and club started

by Benjamin Franklin, constructed the first brownstone in the city for its headquarters in 1814. Subsequently, the flourishing publishing trade moved into the area. Little remains today except Lea and Febiger, which is the country's oldest publishing house, the subsidiary business offices of J.B. Lippincott Company and of the Curtis Publishing Company. At one time, the Curtis Publishing Company and its empire, which included the Saturday Evening Post and Ladies' Home Journal, occupied the huge building on the north side of the square, notable for the 55-foot-long tiffany glass mural in its lobby.

The restoration of Society Hill to the east has encouraged residential building around the square, such as the house of former Mayor Richardson Dilworth, Hopkinson House Apartments, and several additional apartment buildings now under construction at the southeast corner.

The square makes a pleasant starting place for short walks to several interesting areas. Jeweler's Row is a block north on Sansom Street. Pennsylvania Hospital, the oldest in the United States, and the Mikveh Israel Cemetery are a block west at Eighth and Spruce streets. The Walnut Street Theater at Ninth Street, the oldest theater in continuous use in the English-speaking world, was restored to its former elegance in 1971 and is the location of a wide range of film, dance, and theatrical performances. Finally, to the south and east of the square are many outstanding examples of restored colonial houses.

Pennsylvania Hospital, 8th and Spruce

The Atheneum, 6th on Washington Square

Washington Square, 7th and Walnut

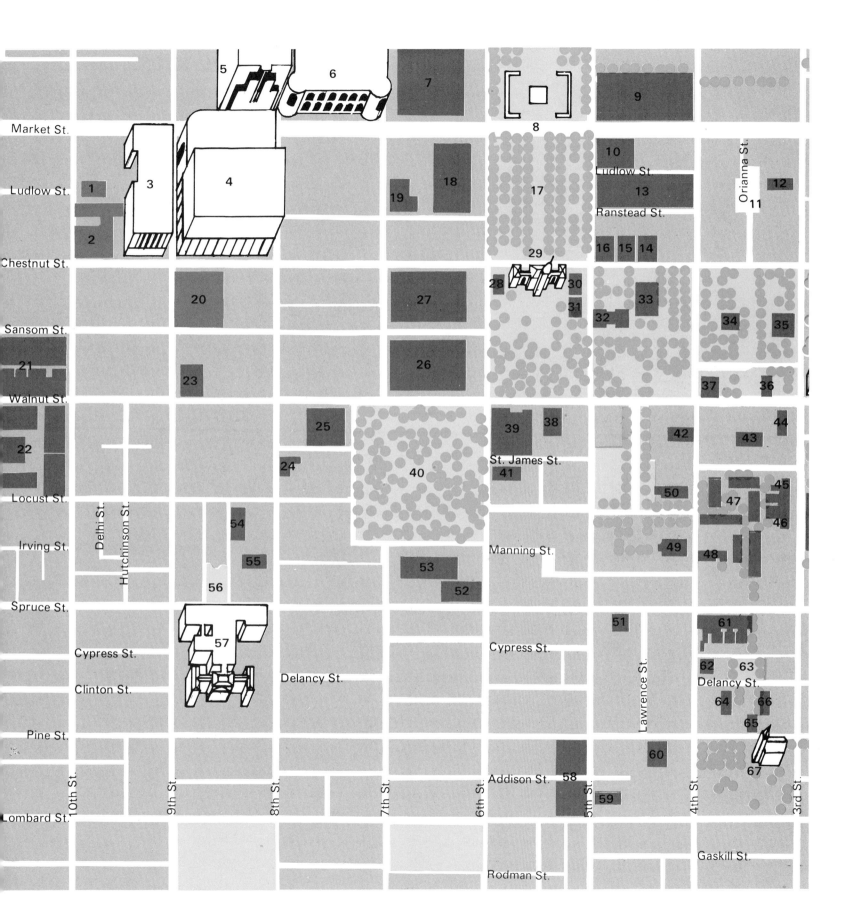

Washington Square

31 American Philosphi-
   cal Society
41 Atheneum
19 Atwater Kent Museum
20 Ben Franklin Hotel
36 Bishop White House
48 Cadwalader House
34 Carpenters Hall
28 Congress Hall
44 Curley Adjustment
   Bureau
26 Curtis Building
63 Delancey Park
 8 Edwin O. Lewis Quad.
64 Evans House
 7 Federal Courthouse
 2 Federal Reserve Bank
35 First Bank of U.S.
11 Franklin Court
 4 Gimbels Dept. Store
61 Girard Row
45 Griffen Houses
53 Hopkinson House
29 Independence Hall
17 Independence Mall
21 Jefferson Hospital
22 Jefferson Med. Col.
62 Hill-Physick-Keith
   House
10 KYW-TV Bldg.
16 Lafayette Building
32 Library Hall
 6 Lit Bros. Dept. Store
15 Maritime Museum
56 Mikveh Israel Ceme-
   tery
54 Musical Fund Hall
30 Old City Hall
38 Penna. Fire Ins.
39 Penn Mutual Life
   Bldg.
57 Pennsylvania Hospital
13 Phila. Bourse Bldg.
42 Phila. Contributor-
   ship Bldg.
14 PNB Bank
 9 PNB Bank Offices
46 Powel House
59 Presbyterian Library
25 PSFS Bank
27 Public Ledger Bldg.
24 Reynolds-Morris
   House
18 Rohm and Haas Bldg.
12 Seamans Church Inst.
33 2nd Bank of the U.S.
50 Shippen Wistar House
51 Society Hill Syna-
   gogue
 5 Strawbridge and
   Clothier
55 St. George's Greek
   Orth. Church
43 St. Joseph's R.C. Ch.
49 St. Mary's Church
67 St. Peter's Church
65 St. Peter's Way
 1 St. Shephen's Church
60 Third Presbyterian Ch.
37 Todd House
58 Town Houses Bower
   and Fradley
47 Town Houses I.M. Pei
52 Trinity R.C. Church
 3 U.S. Post Office and
   Courthouse
23 Walnut St. Theater
40 Washington Square
66 310 Delancey House

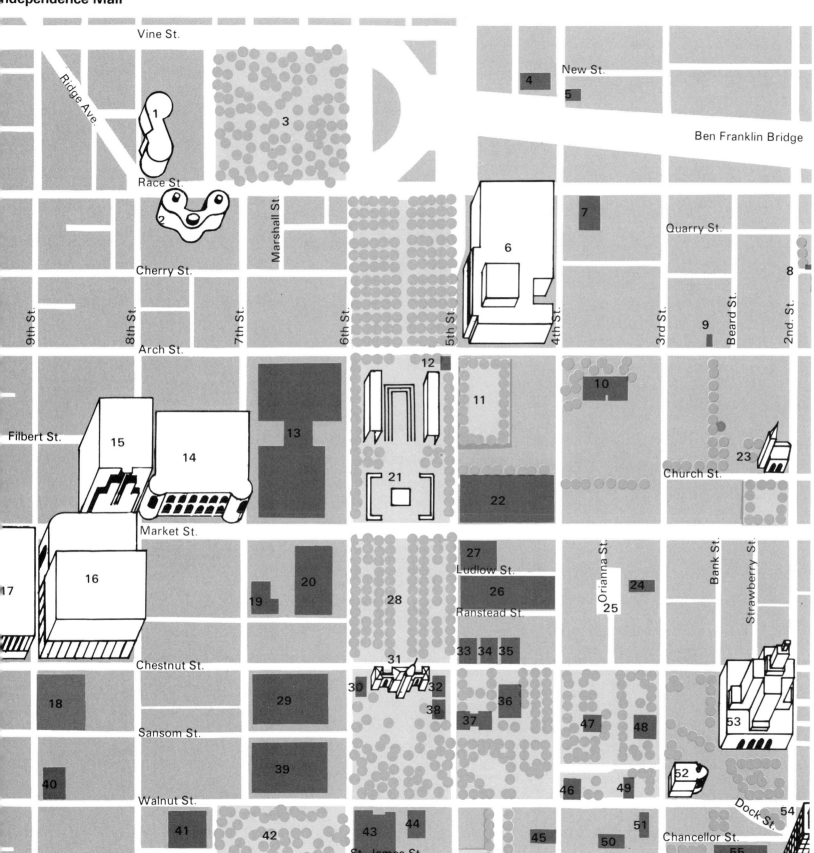

Vine St.

Ridge Ave.

Race St.

Cherry St.

Marshall St.

9th St.

8th St.

7th St.

6th St.

5th St.

4th St.

3rd St.

Beard St.

2nd St.

Arch St.

New St.

Ben Franklin Bridge

Quarry St.

Church St.

Filbert St.

Market St.

Chestnut St.

Ludlow St.

Ranstead St.

Sansom St.

Orianna St.

Bank St.

Strawberry St.

Walnut St.

Dock St.

Chancellor St.

St. James St.

1 2 3 4 5 6 7 8 9 10 11 12 13 14 15 16 17 18 19 20 21 22 23 24 25 26 27 28 29 30 31 32 33 34 35 36 37 38 39 40 41 42 43 44 45 46 47 48 49 50 51 52 53 54 55

50

Independence Mall
before Redevelopment

Independence Mall was
built in three phases:
demolition for the
first, from Market
to Chestnut streets,
was begun in 1952,
and construction was
completed in 1954.
The original fountain
on the north side of
Market Street followed
in 1957. The third
section, the block be-
tween Arch and Race
streets, was completed
in 1963. Finally, the
block between Market
Street and Arch Street,
which contains an
underground parking
garage topped by a
public forum with
thirteen arcades, was
completed in 1967.
The construction of
the bronze Judge
Lewis fountain in
1969 completed the
project.

The Benjamin Franklin
Bridge was opened in
1926 and renamed in
1956 on the 250th anni-
versary of Franklin's
birth. It is 1.8 miles in
overall length, with a
main span of 1,750 feet,
and carries over 25 million
cars per year.

Independence Mall
and National Historical Park

Independence Hall, built from 1734 to 1754, was used as the State House of Pennsylvania until the Second Continental Congress met there in 1775 and 1776. It was the site of the adoption and reading of the Declaration of Independence. During the Revolutionary War it was alternately used by the British as a jail and by the colonists as the seat of Congress. After the war it and the adjacent Congress Hall became the headquarters of the federal government and were finally returned to the city in 1818.

Independence Square was purchased in 1770 and initially landscaped in 1784. The square was restored in 1875 for the Centennial Celebration and again in 1916. During its history Independence Hall has also undergone many restorations. The building was restored in 1828 when William Strickland added the present tower, replacing the earlier one that was found to be unsafe. The National Park Service undertook major restoration starting in 1949 after the area was declared a national historical park. Through its efforts most of the interior rooms have been restored, and millions of visitors pass through the building each year to visit the Liberty Bell.

The three-block area to the east was included in the national park, and over two hundred buildings were demolished (including many significant nineteenth-century buildings), leaving only those civic structures most notable in the early history of the United States. These include Carpenters' Hall, the site of the First Continental Congress; the First and Second banks of the United States; and several outstanding houses such as the Bishop White House, one of the finest restored houses open to the public, and the Todd House, the home of Dolly Madison. The cleared areas have been turned into open parks to provide a setting for these remaining structures.

In 1952 the Commonwealth of Pennsylvania began to clear the area in front of Independence Hall for three blocks to the north. The total project was finished in 1967, after the completion of an underground parking garage and prominent fountain in the central block. The commercial and warehouse buildings adjacent to the mall were cleared by the city through urban renewal. In their place new office buildings have arisen, such as the Rohm and Haas Company headquarters, as well as a new U.S. Mint—a depressing substitute for the fine old building on Spring Garden Street. Several other public and private structures are planned. These include the new Federal Courthouse and Office Building, the Federal Reserve Bank, and KYW-TV's headquarters. The Mikveh Israel Synagogue, designed by Louis I. Kahn extends east along a walkway from the mall to Christ Church.

The major historic colonial sites are all within walking distance of Independence Mall. To the northeast are the Betsy Ross House, where Betsy Ross, who did not make the flag, did not live; Benjamin Franklin's grave in the historic Christ Church Cemetery; the Fighting Quakers' Meeting House; the Fourth and Arch Street Quaker Meeting House; and Elfreth's Alley, reputedly the oldest continuously inhabited residential street in the United States. The numerous nearby museums include the Fire Department Museum near Elfreth's Alley, the Atwater Kent Museum with exhibits on the history of the city, and the Maritime Museum.

A short walk to the south is Society Hill, the most extensive collection of eighteenth-century dwellings in the United States, recently restored through public and private efforts. The observation deck of the Penn Mutual Building behind Independence Hall, open to the public from April to October, provides an excellent view of the entire area.

Franklin Square

Northwest of Independence Mall is Franklin Square, the fourth square originally set aside by William Penn. Named after Benjamin Franklin, this square has fared the least well over the passing years. Like others it was initially a burial ground, then the site of a powder house, and later a public marketplace. For many years it has been surrounded by Philadelphia's skid row and seldom used by any other residents of the city. Recently the Police Administration Building and the Metropolitan Hospital have been constructed adjacent to it, and its character has begun to change. The appearance of the area will deteriorate considerably when the elevated Vine Street Expressway and its connection to the Benjamin Franklin Bridge at the northern edge of the square are completed.

Betsy Ross House, 3rd and Arch

Todd House, 4th and Walnut

First Bank of the United States, Chestnut near 4th

Carpenters' Hall, 4th on Chestnut

United States Mint, 5th and Arch

Bums, Franklin Square

Second Bank of the U.S., Chestnut near 4th

Philadelphia Exchange, 3rd and Walnut

Metropolitan Hospital and Police Administration Building, Franklin Square

The Philadelphia Mint is one of three U.S. mints in the country. The others are in Denver and San Francisco. Its new building on Independence Mall was opened in 1969 to replace the old mint on Spring Garden Street. The new building is the largest mint in the world, having a production capacity of 8 billion coins a year. A glass-enclosed observation gallery within the top floor of the building permits visitors to view the entire coinage operation. Hours: 9:00 A.M. to 3:00 P.M., Monday through Friday.

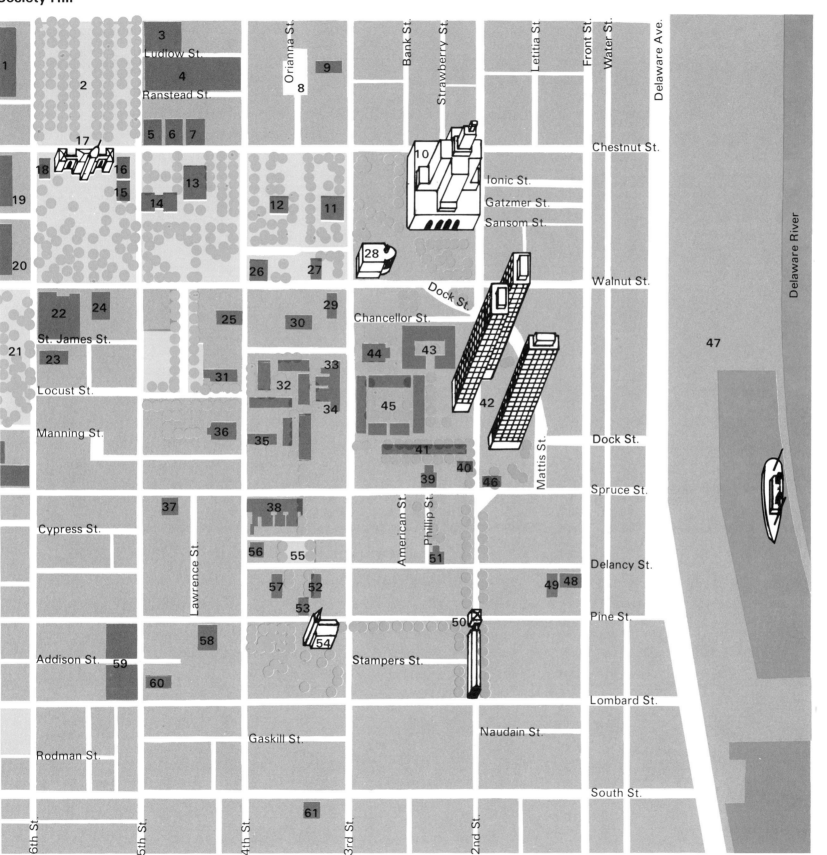

54

Society Hill

Together Society Hill and the adjacent Southwark—Queen Village comprise the oldest section of the city. Society Hill was the first residential area settled in the eighteenth century and in colonial times was also the location of all banking and commerce. The streets were paved with cobblestones in 1761 and many mansions built by wealthy citizens and prominent figures in the revolution. While Philadelphia was the capital of the United States (1790-1800), the President lived near this area.

For the first 150 years, the city was confined largely to Society Hill. However, as development moved westward, the more elegant residential sections moved westward also. More and more warehouses drifted into the historic area so that by the early twentieth century it had become one of the slums of the city. In the 1950s the city attempted to correct this through one of the most expensive urban renewal programs ever undertaken in this country. The area was renamed Society Hill after the Free Society of Traders, a stock company organized by William Penn. (The "Society's Hill" was a parade ground and meeting place during the city's early years.) All significant historic structures were surveyed and identified by the Philadelphia Historical Commission, and almost all others were demolished. The residential structures were acquired by the city and sold to private individuals for accurate restoration. On the cleared lots made available for new residential construction, contemporary design was encouraged.

The city contributed two major public programs to the rehabilitation of the area. One was the removal of the wholesale food center, formerly in a very large area around Dock Street, to a new Food Distribution Center in South Philadelphia. The land was then made available for a high-rise residential complex, the Society Hill Towers, whose developer and design were chosen through a national competition.

The other major contribution was a system of greenways connecting major landmarks and punctuated by a number of small parks and gardens such as the one on Delancey Street between Third and Fourth streets. The greenway network extends south from Independence National Historical Park to St. Peter's Church. A walking tour through the area along this pedestrian way touches most of the historic sites and many of the over 600 historic houses that have been restored.

Society Hill has an abundance of notable colonial churches. Pennsylvania was the only colony with complete religious freedom, so Philadelphia was the only city with churches of all denominations. St. Peter's Church and cemetery was established because Christ Church was too far north for the residents of the area. St. Paul's followed. Old St. Joseph's, St. Mary's (the Catholic cathedral during the Revolution), Old Pine Street Presbyterian, and the Mother Bethel AME Church, founded in 1760 by a freed slave, are all still active.

The Head House Market at Second and Pine streets was built in 1754 to supplement the one on Market Street, although the Head House itself was built as a fire station in 1804. The present building and the shambles or open sheds behind it are typical of the markets that grew up in many other locations throughout the city and were generally removed in the 1880s. Recently the Head House area has been restored as a marketplace with shops and many fine restaurants from French to Greek. Antique shows and craft fairs are held here on weekends during the summer.

Two of the many outstanding houses in Society Hill have been restored with original and period furnishings and opened to the public: the elegant Powel House was once occupied by the mayor of the city, and the Hill-Physick-Keith House is the only freestanding mansion remaining in the area. Several other houses have been restored as museums such as the Man Full of Trouble Tavern and the Perelman Antique Toy Museum (Abercrombie House).

To the south the historic area extends into Southwark, where the first Swedish settlers had located even before Penn's arrival. The area contained a great number of historic houses, but many have been demolished to make way for the Delaware Expressway, and few have been given the public attention and concern those in Society Hill have been fortunate enough to receive. Some of the most interesting houses are on Monroe Street, Kenilworth Street, and Workman Place, where a group of two-and-one-half-story houses dating from 1748 are grouped around a common courtyard. The two most prominent landmarks in the area are Gloria Dei Church, one of the oldest buildings in the city (1700) and the oldest church in Pennsylvania, and the Shot Tower, built in 1808 for the production of rifle shot and thought to be the model for the early lighthouses along the Atlantic coast.

Shot Tower,
2nd and Washington

Dock Street Market
before Redevelopment

Society Hill Towers, 2nd and Locust

Powel House 24 South 3rd

Hill-Physick-Keith House, 4th and Delancey

Town Houses, 2nd and Locust

Head House Square, 2nd and Pine

St. Peter's Walk and Church, Pine between 3rd and 4th

Pei Houses, 3rd and Locust

Head House Square, 2nd and Pine

Old Swedes' Church, Front and Christian

Bingham Court, 4th and Locust

Ben Franklin Bridge from Society Hill Towers

Delancey Park, 4th and Delancey

University City

The area west of the Schuylkill River was purchased from the Indians by William Warner and settled in 1677. At first, only country estates were located in the area then known as Blockley, of which the Woodlands in Woodlands Cemetery is the outstanding example. Development was slow due to difficulty in crossing the river from Philadelphia, until completion of the first permanent bridge in 1805, at that time the longest covered bridge in the world.

By 1840 the area began to be known as West Philadelphia, and the land was subdivided for development. Several great roads radiated from the foot of the Market Street Bridge and were the lines of growth. In 1852 the Pennsylvania Railroad bought the land on the west side of the river, once a burial ground and later the site of the Powelton Fairgrounds. A station was built and later replaced for the Centennial Exposition. The University of Pennsylvania came in 1872. Founded by Ben Franklin in 1751, it was first located at Fourth and Arch streets. It was designated a university in 1779—first in the colonies—and had the first medical school.

The area west of Thirty-second Street to Fortieth Street is called University City and has the greatest concentration of institutions in the city. In addition to the University of Pennsylvania there are the University of Pennsylvania, Children's, Philadelphia General, and Presbyterian Hospitals, Drexel University, and the city's Civic Center and Commercial Museum with exhibits on the growth of the city and the commerce and culture of other nations. The University Museum, adjacent to the Civic Center, has outstanding collections of archaeological finds from many civilizations and is one of the few museums of its kind in the country.

To the north are the University City Science Center and the West Philadelphia Science High School, an outstanding new public school. Though this area seems unexciting as an overall environment, there are a surprisingly large number of buildings designed by distinguished architects. Some of the best are on the Penn Campus such as the Frank Furness Library (now the Graduate School of Fine Arts), Louis I. Kahn's Richards Medical Building, Eero Saarinen's Women's Dormitory, Bower and Fradley's International House, Mitchell/Giurgola's University Museum addition, and their two university parking garages. Powelton Village, slightly north of the Penn campus, boasts a great many interesting Victorian houses fronting on tree-lined streets. Students, professors, and a diverse mix of professionals and average citizens give the area a distinct personality, almost unique in the city.

Furness Library, 34th and Walnut

International House, Chestnut near 38th

Moore School, 33rd and Walnut

Richards Medical Center, 26th and Hamilton Walk

Parking Garage, Walnut at 32nd

Parking Garage, South and 31st

University City
45 Annenberg Communications School
4 Applied Mechanics Research Lab.
7 Armory
13 Centennial Natl. Bank
57 Children's Hospital
50 College Hall
63 Commercial Museum
46 Dietrich Hall
17 Drexel Activities Ctr.
12 Drexel Inst. Main Bldg.
9 Evening Bulletin Bldg.
33 Fels Institute
8 Food Fair Building
27 Franklin Building
60 Franklin Field
49 Furness Library
30 Gimbel Gymnasium
48 Grad. Sch. of Fine Arts
28 Graduate Residence Halls
44 Graduate Sch. of Ed.
32 Harnwell House
34 Harrison House
24 Hill Hall
31 High Rise North
52 Houston Hall
19 Ice Skating Rink
29 International House
51 Irvine Auditorium
25 Law School
16 Library Ctr. (Drexel)
15 Matheson Hall (Drexel)
54 Men's Dormitories
23 Moore Engineering School
20 Palestra
18 Parking Garage
61 Parking Garage
64 Phila. Civic Center
56 Phila. General Hospital
26 Potter Hall
1 Powelton Village
2 Presbyterian Medical Center
43 Psychology Building
55 Richard's Medical Research
6 Rush Building
37 School of Medicine
42 Social Sciences Ctr.
35 St. Mary's Church
14 Stratton Hall
21 Tennis Courts
10 30th Street Station
22 Towne Building
3 University City High School
5 University City Science Center
58 University Hospital
62 University Museum
11 U.S. Post Office
40 V.A. Hospital
36 Van Pelt House
47 Van Pelt Library
41 Veterinary School and Hospital
59 Weightman Hall
53 Wistar Institute
39 Woodland Cemetery
38 Woodland Terrace

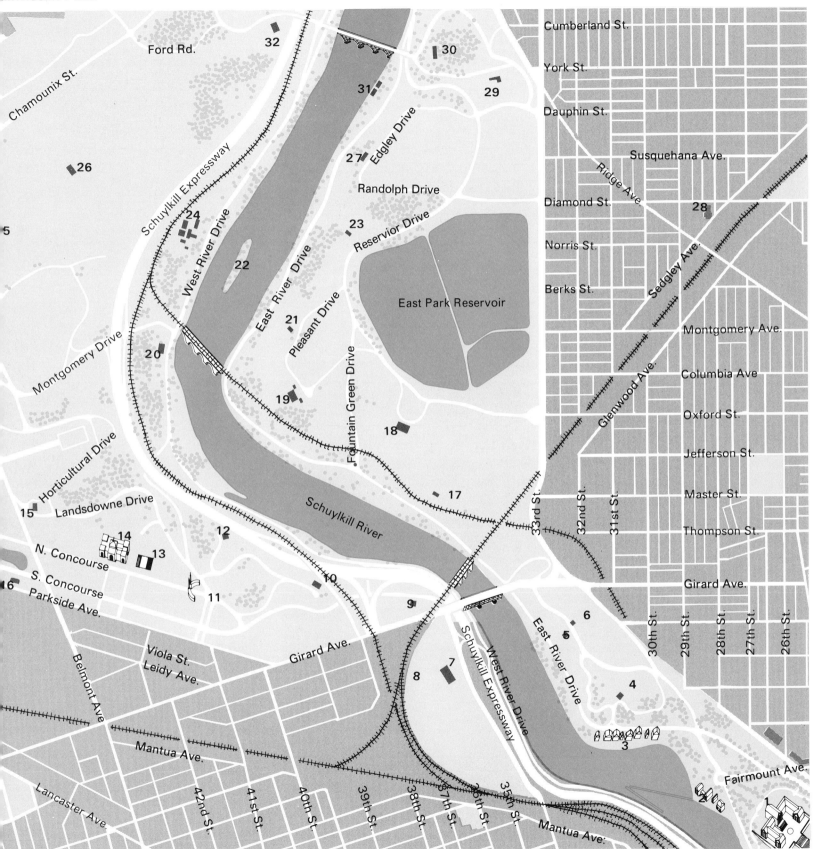

Fairmount Park

Fairmount Park is the largest municipal landscaped park in the United States, covering 4,100 acres mainly along the Schuylkill River and Wissahickon Creek. The park originated in 1812 when the city acquired five acres of Morris Hill, designated as Faire Mount on early maps, for the municipal waterworks and reservoir. The waterworks were built in 1823 and the Fairmount Dam created to run the pumps that raised water to the reservoir. The reservoir has been replaced by the Art Museum, but the waterworks buildings—with original equipment intact—can still be seen along the river behind the museum. The park was expanded in 1844 to protect the water supply and officially created by city ordinance in 1855. A major impetus to its expansion was the 1876 U.S. Centennial Exposition. The first exposition held in the United States, it attracted a great number of visitors to the city and was considered very successful. Memorial Hall, the only one of its major buildings still standing, is the headquarters of the Fairmount Park Commission.

Much of the park land was put together from private country estates, and many of the colonial mansions have been retained throughout the park and are open to visitors. Lemon Hill, Mt. Pleasant, Woodford, and Strawberry Mansion in the East Park, and Sweetbriar in the West Park are probably the most interesting and are expertly restored and furnished. Two mansions have been converted to other uses: Belmont Mansion to a summer restaurant and Chamounix to a youth hostel and meeting place. Other structures of interest are the boat clubs built along the river in the 1890s adjacent to the city waterworks and a traditional Japanese house originally exhibited at the Museum of Modern Art and now situated in a Japanese garden near Memorial Hall.

The park contains recreational facilities of all types, including tennis courts, baseball fields, and natural areas for picnicking. Belmont Plateau is the site of outdoor summer rock concerts, the amphitheater at Robin Hood Dell is the location for more traditional free summer concerts with performers from the Philadelphia Orchestra, and the Playhouse in the Park gives theatrical performances.

The Philadelphia Zoological Garden at the southern end of the park was the first in the United States (1876). A monorail ride covers the entire zoo, and there is a special children's zoo where visitors can walk among and feed the uncaged animals. The Hummingbird House indoor tropical garden with birds flying freely over the visitor's head is one of the outstanding new buildings.

Waterworks behind the Art Museum

Memorial Hall, 48th and Parkside

The first international exposition in the United States was held in Philadelphia in 1876 for the Centennial Celebration of the Declaration of Independence on a site of 236 acres in West Fairmount Park. It was opened by President Grant and the Emperor of Brazil and attended by nearly 10 million people. It was the first exposition to use individual national pavilions, and among its exhibits was Alexander Graham Bell's telephone. Memorial Hall is the only one of its major buildings still standing.

Schuylkill Sculler

Boat Clubs
Bachelors Barge Club 1853
University Boat Club 1854
Undine Boat Club 1856
Quaker City Boat Club 1858
Malta Boat Club 1860
Penna. Boat Club 1861
Phila. Boat Club 1862
Vesper Boat Club 1865
Crescent Boat Club 1867
College Boat Club of University of Pennsylvania

Cedar Grove in Fairmount Park

Mt. Pleasant in Fairmount Park

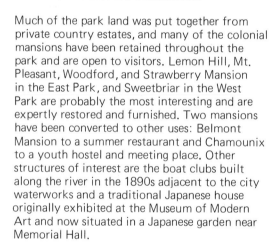

Strawberry Mansion in Fairmount Park

Sweetbriar in Fairmount Park

Lemon Hill in Fairmount Park

Woodford in Fairmount Park

Henry Avenue Bridge, Wissahickon Valley

One of the park's most interesting recreational spots is the Smith Memorial Playground in the East Park, a Victorian recreation center for children, which has as one of its features a sliding board wide enough for ten children side by side. There is also a ten-mile bike path through the park and crew races and sailing on the river throughout the summer.

The Wissahickon Valley was incorporated into the northern portion of the park in 1872. In contrast to the rest, these 1,300 acres are maintained in a natural state with heavily wooded slopes and craggy banks lining the Wissahickon Creek. The six-mile-long Wissahickon Drive following the creek is one of the most scenic routes in the city. Within this portion of the park there are horse and hiking trails, the only covered bridge remaining in a large U.S. city (Thomas Mill Road Bridge), and the Valley Green Inn, the last descendant in Philadelphia of the early wayside inns. Here you can feed the ducks, ride horseback, and have a wonderful Sunday breakfast.

Strawberry Mansion Bridge

Falls Bridge

East Falls Bridges

East Falls Bridges

Germantown and Chestnut Hill

In 1683 Germantown was sold by William Penn to Daniel Pastorius and a group of Dutch and German Quakers. Germantown grew independently of Philadelphia, with its own language and industry, its own customs and style of architecture. James Logan, Secretary to William Penn, built the first "summer" house there, Stenton Mansion, in 1734. Others followed, drawn to the cooler and higher land for summer living. A wealthy merchant, John Wister, built Grumbelthorpe in 1744, and in 1763 Benjamin Chew built Cliveden, the most elegant eighteenth-century house in the area. The yellow fever epidemic of 1793 caused more Philadelphians to flee to Germantown. President Washington was among those who moved on a temporary basis, using the Deshler-Morris House—now restored by the National Park Service—as his summer residence for two years. Many others remained permanently, and Germantown grew rapidly thereafter.

Present-day Germantown Avenue was originally a cart road and became a stage line after 1763. Even before being paved in 1840, it was a commercial street and served the farms that covered the area. Many historic sites still exist along it, including the Old Market Square and a large number of houses built in the typical Germantown style with local stone and prominent white lime joints.

The real impetus for development came with the introduction of the railroads. The first railroad line to Germantown and Chestnut Hill was completed by the Reading in 1854 and was followed in 1884 by the Pennsylvania. Chestnut Hill prospered substantially during this time under the sponsorship of Henry Houston, then President of the Pennsylvania Railroad. Houston built St. Martin in the Fields Church, the present Chestnut Hill Academy; gave land for the Philadelphia Cricket Club and Wissahickon Park; and built 80 to 100 houses of great distinction throughout the area.

Today Germantown is one of the city's most varied residential areas. Its population is almost equally black and white and is one of the most successfully integrated communities in the country. The residential areas contain early mansions such as Cliveden; exotic Victorian houses; interesting collections of small train stations, some by Frank Furness; innovative public housing in the Morton area; and an outstanding collection of contemporary houses by Philadelphia's most prominent architects including Louis I. Kahn, Venturi and Rauch, Mitchell/Giurgola, and others.

Germantown Avenue

Cliveden, 6400 Germantown

Venturi House

Esherick House

Alden Park Manor, School House Lane and Chelten

Germantown Cricket Club, Manheim and Morris

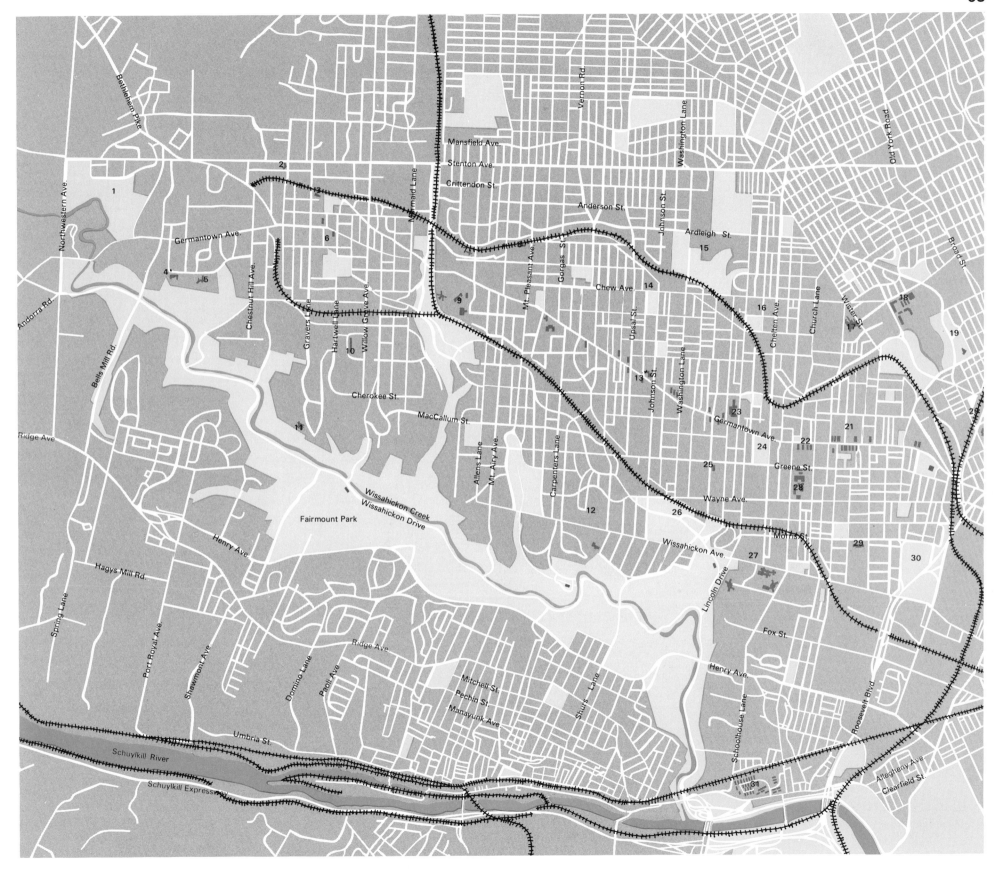

City and Regional Data

The routes and areas describe the city as it is today. But this present form is the result of development and change over a long period of time and is subject to a variety of influences. Population expansion and movement, street growth and urbanization, regional transportation— all influence the present form of the city. This form is, in turn, controlled through a series of legal and political districts that are designed to help it function and to provide the complex range of services required by the population.

1776

1800

1825

1850

1875

1900

1925

1950

1976

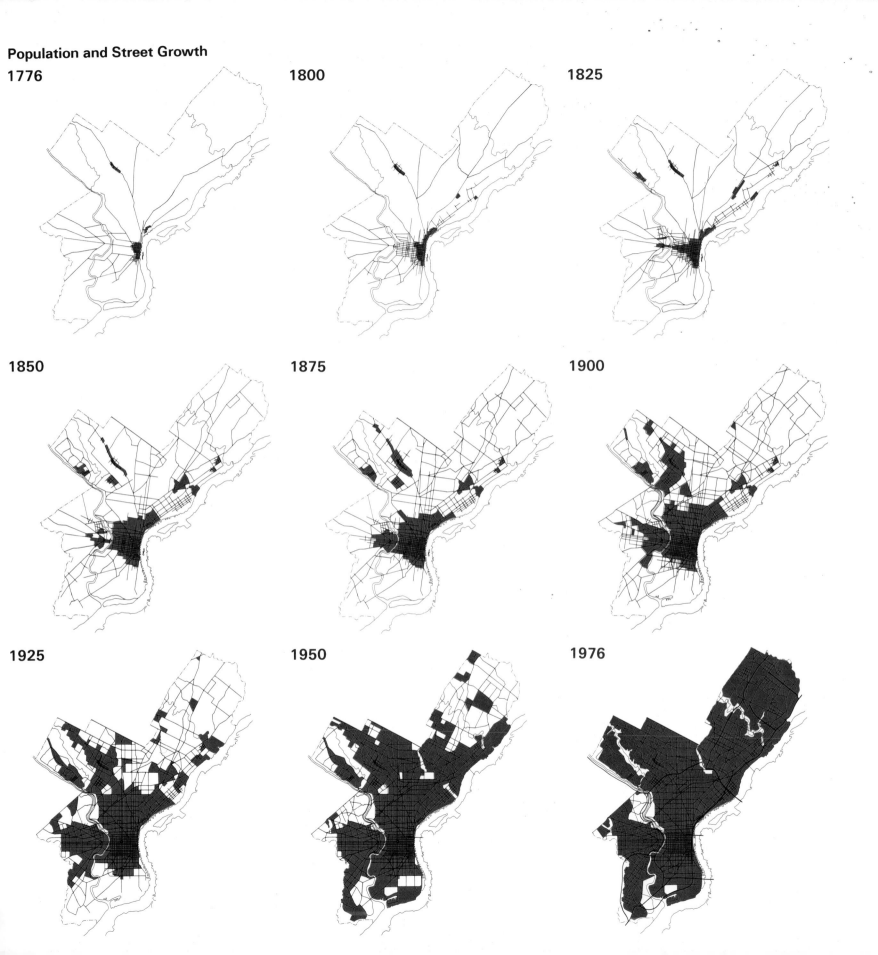

Population Growth

Year	Original City	Balance of County	Suburban Counties	Philadelphia Metropolitan Area Total	Year
1790	28,522	25,869	117,208	171,599	1790
1800	41,216	39,793	134,184	215,193	1800
1810	53,722	57,722	161,127	272,337	1810
1820	63,802	71,835	184,789	320,426	1820
1830	80,458	108,339	212,922	401,719	1830
1840	93,665	164,372	230,923	488,960	1840
1850	121,376	287,386	288,799	697,541	1850
1860	565,022		341,884	907,413	1860
1870	674,022		384,550	1,058,572	1870
1880	847,170		448,962	1,296,132	1880
1890	1,046,964		532,829	1,579,793	1890
1900	1,293,697		598,431	1,892,128	1900
1910	1,549,008		719,201	2,268,209	1910
1920	1,823,779		890,492	2,714,271	1920
1930	1,950,961		1,186,079	3,137,040	1930
1940	1,931,334		1,268,303	3,199,637	1940
1950	2,071,605		1,599,443	3,671,048	1950
1960	2,002,512		2,340,385	4,342,897	1960
1970	1,948,609		2,872,306	4,820,915	1970

1970 Philadelphia Population Characteristics

Age	0-6	7-20	21-44	45-65	over 65	all ages
male	114,974	235,957	270,201	205,645	91,423	1,030,436
female	112,641	237,659	298,690	244,721	136,725	918,173
total	227,588	473,616	568,891	450,366	228,148	1,948,609

Race

white	1,278,717
black	653,719
other	16,101

illiam Penn established the city of Philadelphia
1682, on the western bank of the Delaware
iver, about five miles north of its confluence
ith the Schuylkill. The first settlement was
uickly linked to other nearby, older villages
f Swedish, Dutch, Welsh, and German origins
y the basic road network that was to guide
he future development of the city.

rom its central point on the Delaware at High
treet (Market Street) the city grew outward,
uided by the great highways that led from the
ity to its suburbs and beyond: Moyamensing
nd Passyunk Roads in South Philadelphia;
altimore Turnpike to the southwest; Market
treet and the Lancaster Turnpike to the west;
he Ridge Road and Germantown Turnpike to
he northwest; and the New York Post Road
Frankford Turnpike) to the northeast.

Vhile Penn's grant covered 26,000,000 acres,
he original city of Philadelphia was only in the
rea between Vine and South streets, between
he Delaware and Schuylkill rivers, covering
pproximately two square miles. The first official
J.S. Census in 1790, counted 28,522 persons in
hat area, most of them in the blocks along the
Delaware surrounding the nation's capital. Along
he river above the city was the emerging working
lass suburb called the Northern Liberties District,
nd below was the Southwark District. Out-
ying communities such as Kingsessing (south-
vest), Blockley (west), German Township (north-
vest), and Frankford (northeast) had an inde-
endent existence some miles outside the city.

he population growth was so rapid that by 1850
here were more than 121,000 persons in the
wo-square-mile city, with more than 287,000
n the outlying districts, boroughs, townships,
nd villages of Philadelphia County. In 1854 the
ounty and the city were consolidated into a
ingle political jurisdiction which, at the outbreak
f the Civil War in 1860, had reached 565,529
ersons.

During the early decades of industrialization
1820 to 1880), immigrants from Ireland,
England, Scotland, Wales, Germany, and other
orthern and western European countries
rrived to work in the city's shops, docks, mills,
nd farms. By 1890 the population had reached
,046,964, and the built-up area had swallowed
p most of the old towns and villages of the
ounty.

While it had taken about 200 years to reach its
first million, in only 50 years a second million
was added to the city's population. Beginning
in the 1800s, huge demands for labor in the
production mills and assembly factories brought
new thousands of immigrants from the peasant
villages of southern and eastern Europe and, in
the twentieth century, from the rural American
South.

As Italians, Russians, Poles, diverse other Slavs,
Austrians, Hungarians, and others poured into
the country, the U.S. Congress reacted in alarm.
Following the "red scares" at the conclusion of
World War I, severe restrictions were imposed
upon immigration from these "nontraditional"
nations.

After the mid-1920s, owing to such legislation,
foreign immigration became a less important
source of city and regional growth. The depressed
1930s and the war-torn early 1940s substantially
reduced the flow of white Europeans, but a large
influx of black immigrants came from the South
Atlantic and Deep South states.

By 1920 the city's population had reached
1,823,779. Thereafter it grew slowly and remained at about 2,000,000 for almost 40 years
until 1970, when it dipped lower than it had
been since 1930. Although the change in the
total population of the city over the past four
decades had been slight, there has been considerable change in the distribution of that population. The older residential inner-city areas have
thinned out considerably and been converted to
commercial, industrial, and institutional uses,
while outlying sections have been increasingly
more thickly settled and are now almost completely developed.

After the First World War the surrounding suburban counties witnessed dramatic population
growth. This ring of counties (Bucks, Montgomery, Delaware, and Chester in Pennsylvania
and Gloucester, Camden, and Burlington in New
Jersey) contained 890,492 persons in 1920 and
had more than tripled to 2,847,297 in 1970.

Ethnic Growth

Questions on race and national origin have been
asked in every census since 1790; but only for
the censuses of 1910, 1930, and 1960 were data
published on the geographic distribution of the
foreign stock (foreign-born persons and native-
born of foreign parentage) within the city. The
census has not inquired beyond parentage, and
to a rather substantial degree the second gene-
ration of immigrant offspring has lost its distinctive ethnic identification in the melting pot of
white America. Blacks, however, have been identified in each census as a distinct racial group.

The maps on the succeeding pages graphically
portray the location and magnitude of the main
ethnic groups in Philadelphia in 1910, 1930,
and 1960. Note the large numbers and wide dis-
persal of the early immigrant groups (from Ireland, the United Kingdom, and Germany) in
1910, their considerable diminution by 1960,
and their outward movement into the new
neighborhoods of the southwest, northwest, far
north, and northeast—following the pattern of
the city's expansion and development.

Then note the later immigrants (from Russia,
Poland, Italy, Austria, Hungary) who settled
in great density in the old neighborhoods along
the Delaware River, grew even larger in numbers
and expanded in area by 1930, often establishing new secondary communities in middle-aged
neighborhoods, and began to diminish in population by 1960. In some cases their earlier
areas of residence were completely abandoned
as this segment of the population followed
the developing city into the outlying areas and
into the suburbs.

Note finally the large and steady increase of
blacks in the city. The black community in
Philadelphia had grown gradually to more than
84,000 persons in 1910. The main concentration of this population was in the south central
area west of Broad Street, in some of the older
inner-city areas of West and North Philadelphia,
and in central Germantown. In the next 20 years
the black population grew to almost 220,000
persons, and their predominant areas of residence
in the city had spread westward, northward,
and slightly to the east.

In the next 30 years, blacks more than doubled
in population again, numbering 529,000 by
1960 and 654,000 by 1970. One in three residents of the city is now black, but this huge
segment of the population is still relatively com-
pacted into areas of South Central Philadelphia;
West Philadelphia along the Market Street Axis;
North Philadelphia, which alone has a black
population of 300,000 and is the Model Cities
area; and Northwest Philadelphia (Tioga, Nicetown, Logan, Germantown, and Mount Airy).

City Statistics

130 square miles
550,000 buildings
2.650 miles of street
(Longest street: Roose-
velt Boulevard, 12.3
miles; longest straight
street: Broad Street,
11.8 miles)

Ethnic Growth

1910

1930

1960

Italian

Irish

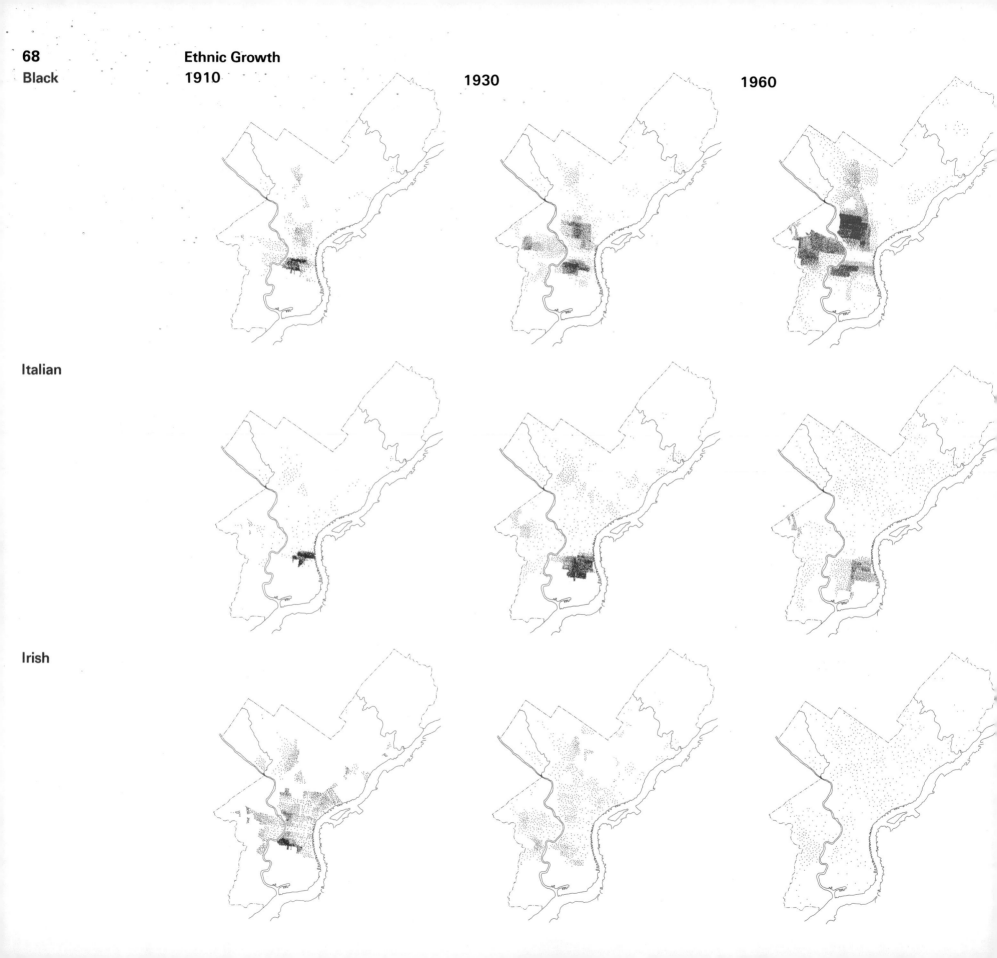

1910   1930   1960

English
Canadian

German
Austrian

Russian
Polish

Legal and Political Districts

When the city and county were consolidated in 1854, Philadelphia was divided into wards based on old county townships or districts. Most present districts are based on population and make use of this division of the city by ward. Though formal boundaries have been forgotten, many township names are still used to designate neighborhoods, such as Kennsington, Mayfair, Pennsport, or Moyamensing. But while population changed, the ward boundaries were not revised until 1965 when a realignment commission was established to attempt to make the wards approximately equal in population.

There are now 66 wards in Philadelphia ranging in population from 13,000 to 54,000, but with the majority containing from 20,000 to 30,000. Each ward has two representatives to the city committee of both major political parties, through which the political views of the citizenry are supposed to be represented. Ward boundaries were used to determine census tracts when they were informally drawn up in 1930. Formally adopted in 1940, census tracts were intended to cover homogeneous communities and so have become the basis for many other types of districts.

The city uses many districts for administrative purposes, for instance, for postal, school, health, and police services. The Planning Commission has 12 analysis districts, which were established in 1940; there are 10 health districts, 8 school districts, 22 police districts, and 13 fire battalions. Each department claims its facilities can serve a different number of people, so none of the districts has the same boundaries.

In addition there are a variety of political districts. There are 10 council districts of equal population. City charter requires that these boundaries be revised every ten years following the completion of the U.S. Census, or the councilmen's pay stops until the task in done. In addition to district councilmen, there are 7 councilmen-at-large, at least 2 of which must be from minority parties. Their term of office is four years.

Until 1970 Philadelphia had 5 U.S. Congressional districts. Because of the decrease in city population, redistricting was required, and one district was combined with adjacent county areas. Now there are 4 congressional districts of approximately equal population from which members of the U.S. House of Representatives are elected for two-year terms. The same redistricting procedure was required for state senatorial and congressional districts. Philadelphia now has 9 senatorial districts out of 50 in the state, and 35 congressional districts out of 203 in the state. Senators are elected to four-year terms and representatives to two-year terms.

Blue Laws governing Sunday activities originated in New Haven, Connecticut. The Philadelphia law dates from a state statute of 1794 still in effect and prohibits "any worldly employment or business whatsoever on the Lord's Day." The statute was amended in 1922 to allow baseball, football, and fishing; in 1939 to allow movies and concerts; in 1967 to allow businessmen who recognize and close on another day to remain open on Sunday; and in 1971 to permit sale of alcoholic beverages in restaurants.

Philadelphia Neighborhoods

1 Academy Gardens	40 Lawndale	78 Strawberry Mansion
2 Andorra	41 Lexington Park	79 Tacony
3 Angora	42 Logan	80 The Neck
4 Awbury	43 Ludlow	81 Tioga
5 Belmont	44 Manayunk	82 Torresdale
6 Brewerytown	45 Mantua	83 University City
7 Bridesburg	46 Mayfair	84 West Mount Airy
8 Burhlome	47 Modena Park	85 West Oak Lane
9 Bustleton	48 Morrell Park	86 West Philadelphia
10 Castor Area	49 Mount Airy	87 Winchestar Park
11 Center City	50 Nicetown	88 Wissahickon
12 Chestnut Hill	51 Normandy	89 Wissinoming
13 Chinatown	52 Northeast Industrial	90 Wynnefield
14 Crescentville	Park	
15 East Falls	53 North Philadelphia	
16 East Germantown	54 Northwood	
17 East Oak Lane	55 Ogontz	
18 Eastwick	56 Olney	
19 Elmwood	57 Overbrook	
20 Fairhill	58 Overbrook Park	
21 Far Northeast	59 Oxford Circle	
22 Feltonville	60 Packer Park	
23 Fern Rock	61 Parkwood Manor	
24 Fishtown	62 Pennypack Woods	
25 Fox Chase	63 Pleasant Hill	
26 Francisville	64 Point Breeze	
27 Frankford	65 Powelton Village	
28 Franklinville	66 Rawnhurst	
29 Germantown	67 Richmond	
30 Girard Estate	68 Robindale	
31 Glenwood	69 Roxborough	
32 Haddington	70 Shawmont	
33 Harrowgate	71 Sherwood	
34 Holme Circle	72 Society Hill	
35 Holmesburg	73 Somerton	
36 Hunting Park	74 South Philadelphia	
37 Juniata Park	75 Southwark	
38 Kensington	76 Spruce Hill	
39 Kingsessing	77 Stenton	

State Senate

State House

Councilmanic

Congressional

Wards

Postal Zones

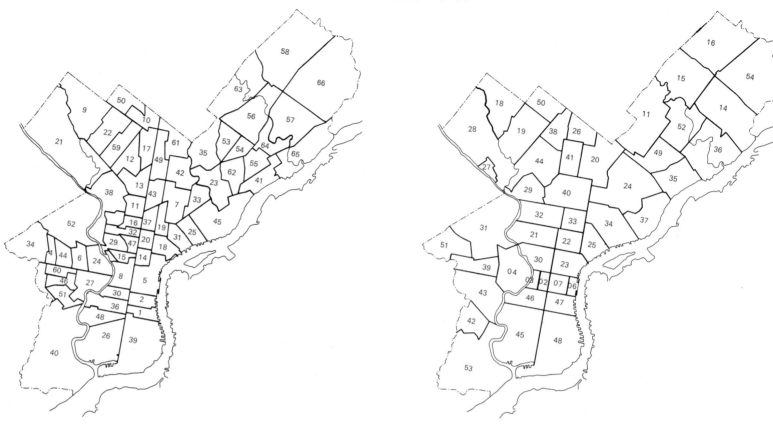

Census Tracts

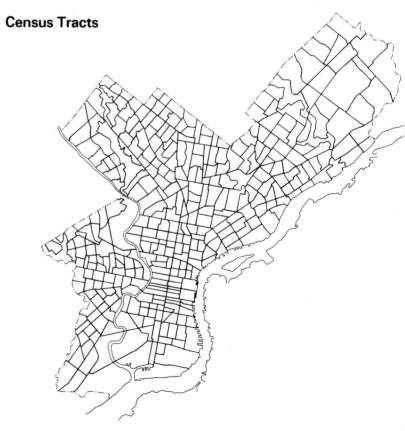

William Penn's plan for Philadelphia was a regional plan that laid out major roads and encouraged development through the sale of townships. Urbanization began around the great roads and then along the railroad lines. By the time the first regional plan was done in 1932, substantial corridors of development extended out from Philadelphia, particularly to the west along the main line of the Pennsylvania Railroad. Intensive urbanization continued to grow outward from Penn's original city and to concentrate along the Delaware River. The port operations—now fourth largest in the United States and one of the largest in foreign tonnage—stimulated industrial development on both sides of the river from Chester to Camden, New Jersey, and north almost to the Philadelphia city limits. In 1969 the Delaware Valley Regional Planning Commission (DVRPC) adopted a plan to further guide the development of the nine-county area.

The Delaware Valley Region consists of Philadelphia and the four Pennsylvania and four New Jersey counties surrounding it. This region covers approximately 3,500 square miles and contains more than four million people.

The Pennsylvania counties are Bucks, Montgomery, Chester, and Delaware. Bucks and Montgomery counties to the north and west were founded in 1682 and 1784, respectively. They are more affluent than Chester and Delaware and are growing more rapidly.

Bucks County covers 617 square miles and has a population of 415,000. The northern boundary is along the Delaware River, and there are many small historic towns, such as Fallsington, and pleasant country drives (thirteen covered bridges) throughout the county, although the area around New Hope is the best known. The eastern half of the county has been developing rapidly, replacing agricultural land with large residential and industrial development. Levittown, the nationally famous housing development, is located here, as is U.S. Steel's Fairless Works, which contains three blast furnaces and is located near Morrisville (free tours are given on Wednesday afternoons). However, the western half of the county remains rural and has attracted many writers-turned-gentlemen-farmers, including James Michener, Pearl S. Buck, and James Gould Cozzens.

Montgomery County is slightly larger (491 square miles) and has a population of 624,000. Urbanization is increasing rapidly and now covers half the county. Impetus has come from industrial growth, particularly in the aerospace industry, for example, General Electric's Missile Guidance Center at Valley Forge. Montgomery County has many excellent residential areas; Jenkintown and Merion townships are inhabited by numerous Philadelphia business leaders, while Bryn Athyn is a unique community consisting almost entirely of Swedenborgians (the Swedenborgian Cathedral and College are well worth a visit).

Chester and Delaware counties to the south and west were founded in 1682 and 1789, respectively. Chester is the largest in area (760 square miles) and the smallest in population (278,000). It is the leading agricultural area with only limited urbanization along the main line of the Penn Central, which runs through the center of the county. Delaware county by contrast is the smallest (185 square miles), yet has the second largest population (601,000). This has created denser development, particularly around the city of Chester, which shares problems of physical decay and racial unrest with Philadelphia and Camden. Some of the region's best schools are in the county, including Swarthmore and Haverford Colleges. Petroleum refining is the major industry, although there are others, such as the Boeing Company's Vertol Division, in the area south of Philadelphia International Airport.

The New Jersey counties are Camden, Burlington, and Gloucester.

Places of Interest and Transportation

The eight counties surrounding Philadelphia contain a wide variety of historic sites and places of interest. The Liberty Trail attempts to connect most of the major places of interest and includes on the route three Revolutionary War sites.

Washington's Crossing State Park marks the place where Washington crossed the Delaware on Christmas Eve, 1776 (an event that is re-enacted each year). The park covers 500 acres along the riverbank. In addition to the Memorial Building with a reproduction of Emanuel Leutze's famous painting of the event, there is an unusual wild-flower preserve and nature center. Valley Forge Park covers the 2,255 acres where Washington's defeated army spent the winter of 1777-1778 training and preparing for the spring offensive. Remains of their encampment and Washington's headquarters exist throughout the park, which is also noted for its hiking trails and 55,000 magnificent dogwood trees.

Brandywine Battlefield to the south is a 50-acre park on the site where General Howe forced Washington to retreat in 1777, allowing the British to occupy Philadelphia.

In the Brandywine area are three places of unusual interest established by the du Pont family. Longwood Gardens, formerly the estate of Pierre S. du Pont, is a horticultural delight. The grounds are covered with a variety of gardens including an Italian water garden. A huge indoor conservatory is open year round, and in summer there are extraordinary fountain displays and concerts. Not far from Longwood Gardens is the recently opened Brandywine Museum in Chadds Ford, which exhibits the work of local painters including Andrew Wyeth. Both should be visited.

Even more delightful is the Henry Francis du Pont Winterthur Museum of American decorative arts from 1640 to 1840, displayed in 100 authentic rooms, which have been removed from early houses and restored and furnished exactly as they were in actual use.

Not far away is another du Pont museum, the Hagley Museum of the history of industry in the United States. Located in an old textile mill, it is focused on early U.S. mills and is adjacent to the first black powder mill in the United States, which was started by the du Ponts in 1804.

There are many other places of interest throughout the region. The Mercer Museum in Doylestown presents the history of American tools in one of the first buildings totally constructed in reinforced concrete. Pennsbury Manor near Bristol on the Delaware River is the reconstructed country estate of William Penn. Andalusia on the Delaware River, Whitemarsh Hall in Wyncote, and the Widener Mansion in Elkins Park are all elegant remnants of the nineteenth century. The Buten Museum in Merion contains the most diversified collection of Wedgwood in the world, and the Campbell Soup Company in Camden, New Jersey, has a fascinating museum of historic soup tureens. The Barnes Foundation is a privately endowed educational institution that owns an extraordinary art collection including a large representation of the work of Renoir, Cézanne, and Matisse. And Alverthorpe in Jenkintown, the home of Mr. and Mrs. Lessing Rosenwald, contains one of the country's leading collections of prints and rare books. All the counties are known for scenic roads, but perhaps Bucks County is most famous, particularly in the area around New Hope.

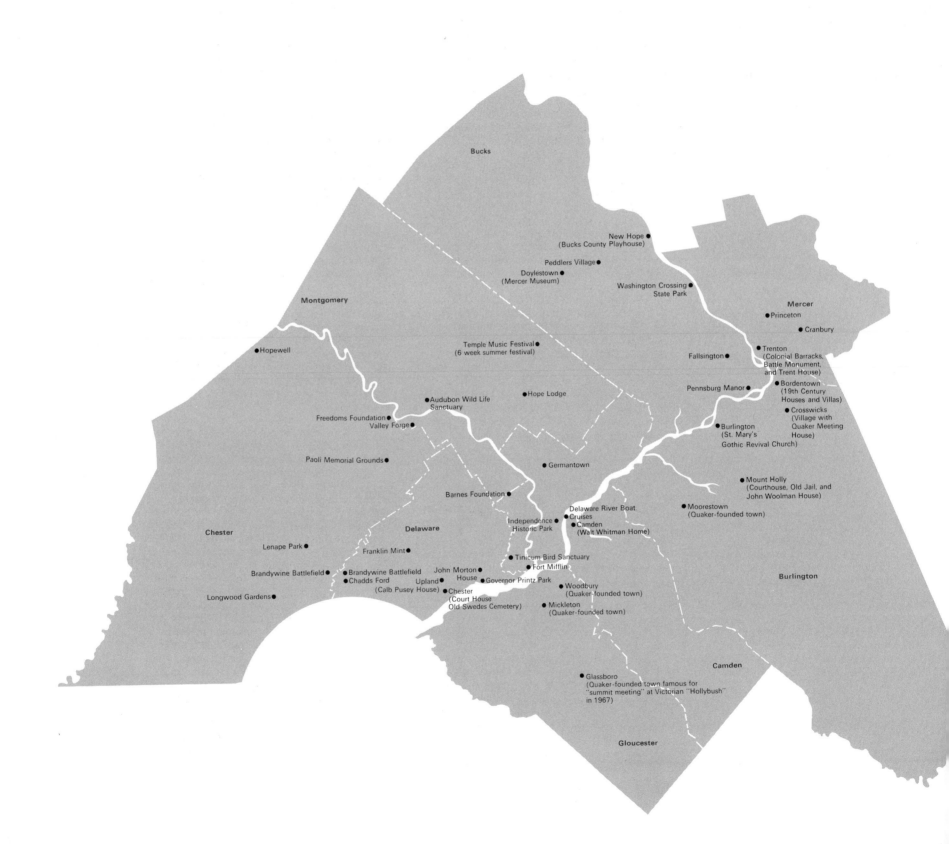

Bucks

New Hope ●
(Bucks County Playhouse)

Peddlers Village ●

Doylestown ●
(Mercer Museum)

Washington Crossing ●
State Park

Montgomery

Mercer

● Princeton

● Cranbury

● Hopewell

Temple Music Festival ●
(6 week summer festival)

Fallsington ●

● Trenton
(Colonial Barracks,
Battle Monument,
and Trent House)

● Audubon Wild Life
Sanctuary

● Hope Lodge

Pennsburg Manor ●

● Bordentown
(19th Century
Houses and Villas)

Freedoms Foundation ●
Valley Forge ●

● Crosswicks
(Village with
Quaker Meeting
House)

Paoli Memorial Grounds ●

● Burlington
(St. Mary's
Gothic Revival Church)

Barnes Foundation ●

● Germantown

● Mount Holly
(Courthouse, Old Jail, and
John Woolman House)

Chester

Delaware

Delaware River Boat
Cruises ●

● Moorestown
(Quaker-founded town)

Lenape Park ●

Independence ●
Historic Park

● Camden
(Walt Whitman Home)

Burlington

Franklin Mint ●

Brandywine Battlefield ●

● Brandywine Battlefield
● Chadds Ford

John Morton ●
House

● Tinicum Bird Sanctuary
● Fort Mifflin

Upland ●
(Calb Pusey House)

● Governor Printz Park

● Woodbury
(Quaker-founded town)

Longwood Gardens ●

● Chester
(Court House
Old Swedes Cemetery)

● Mickleton
(Quaker-founded town)

Camden

● Glassboro
(Quaker-founded town famous for
"summit meeting" at Victorian "Hollybush"
in 1967)

Gloucester

Primary and Major Highways

Limited Access Highways

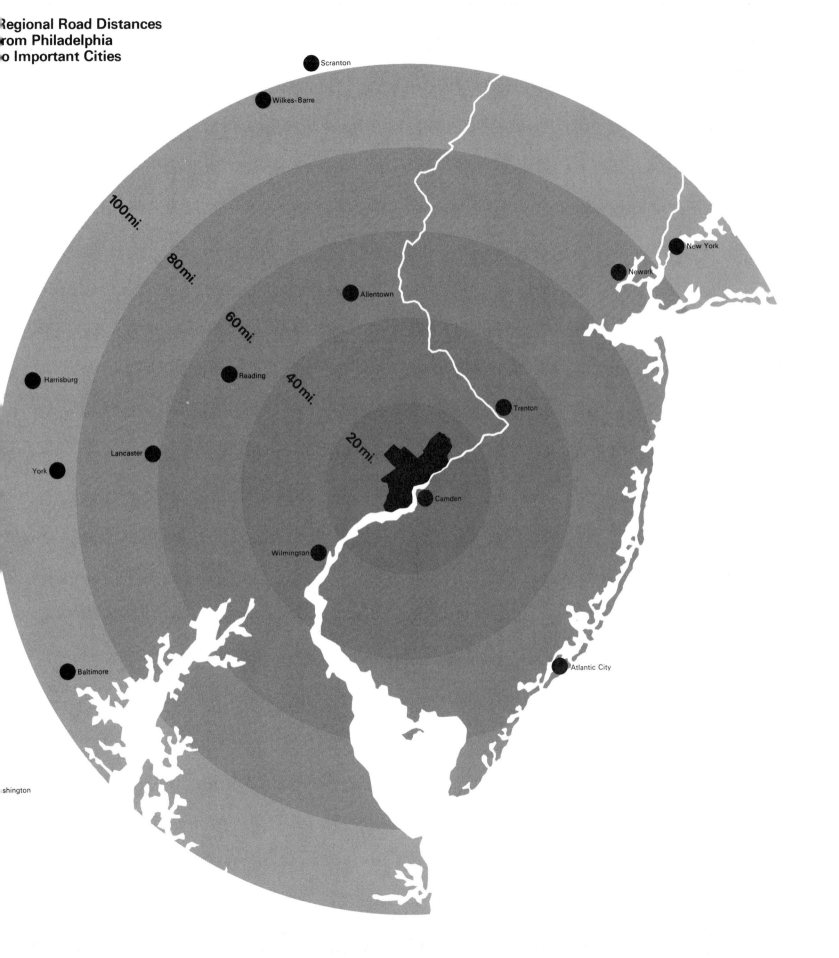

Plans for Philadelphia

Present form and patterns of growth are generally the result of a limited number of consciously developed public policies and plans. Many cities have simply grown without any controls, and the resultant form is dependent upon the network of streets. In all cases the final achievement is the result of work by individual architects who serve the needs of private clients and the public while working within the context of a broader image of the city.

William Penn looked upon his grant of lands in America as an opportunity to conduct a "Holy Experiment." He proposed to found a society based upon justice and tolerance and chose to name the city Philadelphia for its Greek meaning, "City of Brotherly Love."

The original city was located at the narrowest part of the peninsula, between the Delaware and Schuylkill rivers. The plan was laid out for Penn by his surveyor, Thomas Holme, in 1682. The area covered was 1,280 acres, and the boundaries to the north and south were the present Vine and South streets. Holme's plan differed substantially in execution from Penn's initial idea of a green country town with houses set in the middle of large plots of land. Under the influence of military camps and English towns, particularly Londonderry, Holme laid out a rigid grid system of streets. He gave purchasers narrow lots in the city and compensated for this with free lots in the Liberty Lands to the north of the city.

Two main thoroughfares approximately bisected the town, High Street (now Market Street) and Broad Street. At their intersection a center square of ten acres was set aside for the town hall. In the center of each of the four quadrants, eight-acre squares were set aside for the common use and enjoyment of all the citizens.

Penn was a real estate entrepreneur. He offered initial purchase lots along both riverfronts and tried to encourage development to move inward thereby increasing the value of the land he continued to own.

After the revolution all of Penn's land was taken over by the Commonwealth and sold off rather rapidly. The Liberty Lands of North Philadelphia were quickly developed on a speculative basis, with rows of identical builders' houses. In Center City the back alleys designed for service access were declared public streets, which encouraged further subdivision of the small city lots and laid the foundation for present street plan and traffic problems. Small three-story houses with one room per floor (popularly known as "Father-Son-Holy Ghost" houses) were built on the backs of lots in these small alleys, further adding to the problems of congestion.

Cities planned in advance of the construction of the first buildings are comparatively rare. In colonial America, none was as carefully planned as Philadelphia. Beyond the central city Penn was concerned about the connections to other areas and made sure that roads were laid out before the land was divided among the various purchasers.

Penn's Plan 1682

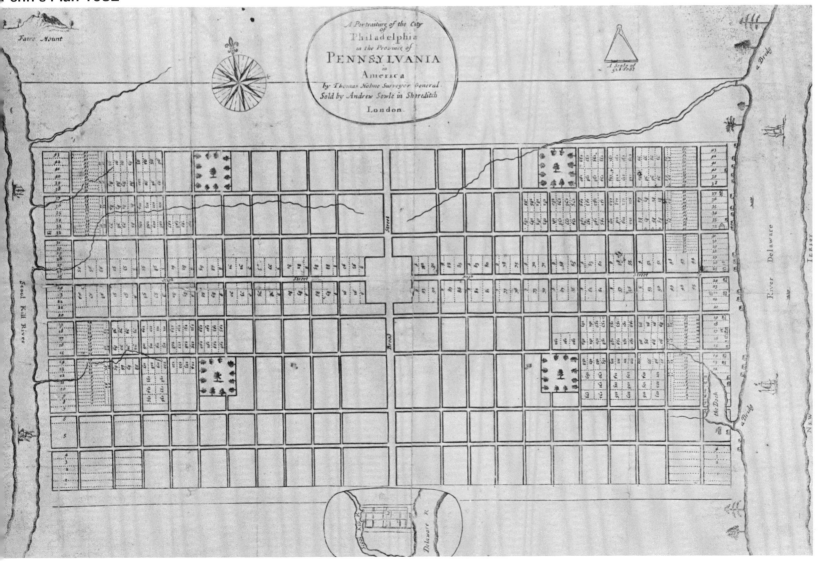

Most of these roads remain in the present plan of
the city. In addition to the Liberty Lands Penn
established eight manors outside the city, given
mainly to his family, to control expansion. To
persons with a similar background, he also sold
townships, generally around 5,000 acres, which
could in turn be sold by lots to individuals. The
most successful of these was Germantown; Radnor,
Merion, and Haverford townships were also started in this way.

Philadelphia grew steadily within the context of
Penn's plan of 1682. The fact that Penn's heirs
continued to hold large pieces of real estate until
1790 almost ensured that his vision would be real-
ized. In succeeding decades few changes were
made, as can be seen in the plan prepared by John
Hill, surveyor and draftsman, in 1796. It was not
until 1960 that a major new plan for Philadelphia was developed under the auspices of the re-
vitalized City Planning Commission.

1796 Plan

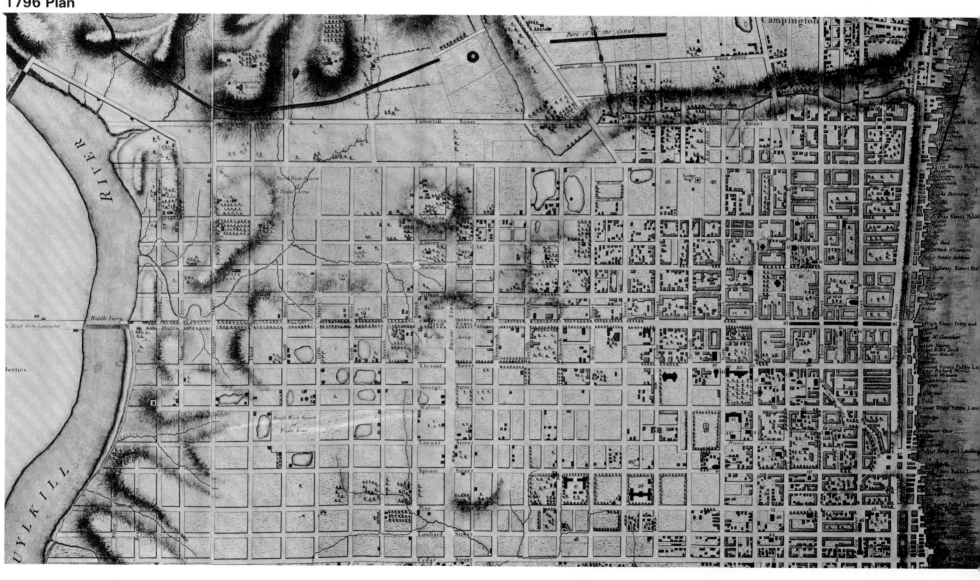

Center City Plan 1960–1963

The City Planning Commission was originally established in the Charter Revision of 1919. By 1931 it had initiated a number of major transportation projects including the Benjamin Franklin Parkway, Schuylkill River Drive, Roosevelt Boulevard (now the longest street in the city), the Benjamin Franklin Bridge, and the Broad Street Subway.

Early planners considered the business of the city to be economic growth and, therefore, concentrated their efforts on Center City and allowed the strictly residential areas to grow haphazardly. When a new interest in planning began in the early 1940s, it also focused on Center City problems. Initial citizen attention concentrated on the decay of the historic areas. By the late 1940s this concern for physical change coincided with a broader concern for governmental reform.

The Better Philadelphia Exhibit of 1949 at Gimbels Department Store (now in the Civic Center Museum) showed Philadelphians what the city could be like. A major part of the exhibit was a model of Center City with moving sections to show new projects. The Revised Charter of 1951 which was in part a response to the exhibit, gave the City Planning Commission new powers, the most important of which was the preparation of six-year capital programs for all city capital expenditures. Under the leadership of the executive director, Edmund N. Bacon, the Planning Commission started to carry out the ideas in the exhibit. A comprehensive plan for the development of the city was approved and adopted in 1960. In 1963 the Planning Commission completed its plan for Center City, covering the same area as William Penn's original plan.

That plan had survived quite well in the intervening 280 years. The City Hall had been built in the Center Square, the four parks were still in their original locations, and urbanization reached from river to river. The one major change was the diagonal slash made by the Benjamin Franklin Parkway cutting across the grid.

The Center City Plan initiated the major projects that have begun to change the appearance of the city: the completion of Penn Center and Independence Mall, the reconstruction of the retail commercial areas (known as Market East), the restoration of Society Hill, the construction of Penn's Landing along the Delaware River, and the provision of new highways and parking facilities.

1960 Plan

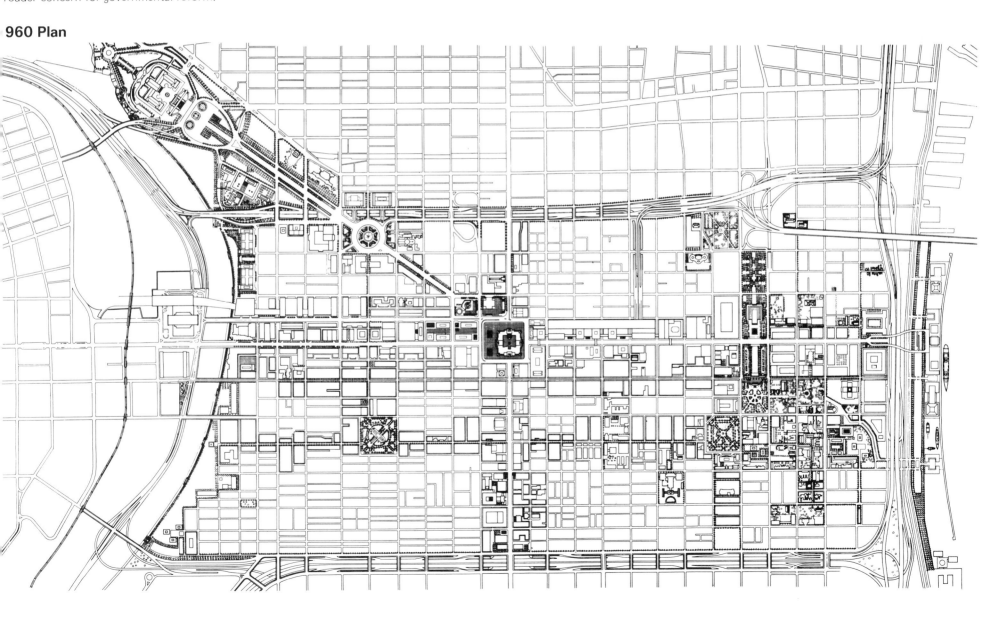

Citizens' Plans 1960–1970

The extensive urban renewal program begun in the 1950s drew many architects to the city and involved them in major projects. Many, however, were as concerned with the total character of the urban environment as the City Planning Commission and expressed that commitment in plans that went beyond concern for single buildings in conception. The Planning Commission had asked Louis I. Kahn to develop ideas for the Market Street East area, and from this beginning Kahn gradually expanded his work to consider all of Center City. Under a grant from the Graham Foundation, he developed a series of ideas including a hierarchical pattern of street movements, coupled with a system of parking garages (harbors).

While few of the ideas in Kahn's plan found their way into public policies, his personal Philadelphia plan provided a precedent for many young designers in the late 1960s when the city began considering ideas for a major celebration in 1976. At least eight citizen groups produced plans for the location of bicentennial activities or for an international exposition. The Committee for an International Exposition in Philadelphia in 1976 produced a plan for the Thirtieth Street area, which was subsequently adopted as public policy but was then succeeded by a series of other plans developed by the Philadelphia 1976 Bicentennial Corporation.

A Center City Plan by Louis Kahn

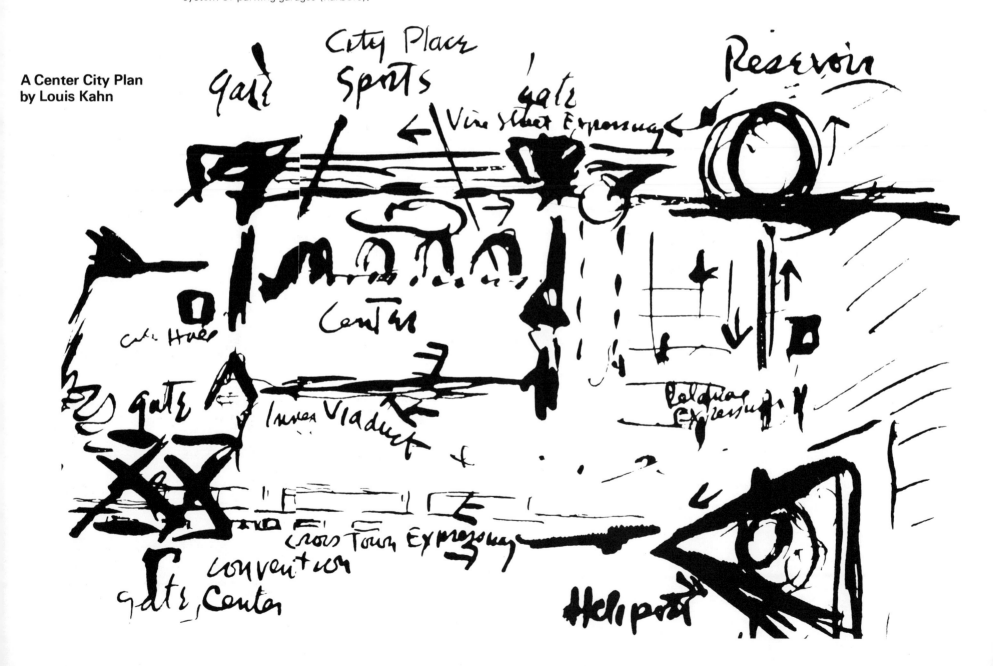

Center City Plan 1972

The Center City Plans of 1960-1963 indicated preliminary ideas for the major downtown projects. By 1972 these plans had changed considerably; nevertheless, many original projects are now complete. Others have undergone substantial redesign and are now nearing construction, but almost all of the projects identified in 1960-1963 can be seen in one stage or another throughout Center City. Many that were not identified in the early plan have developed as a result of publicly initiated projects. These include the Hahnemann and Jefferson Medical Centers, Washington Square West residential community renewal, and the Franklin Town Project. Only one major project of the 1960-1963 plan—the Market East Transportation Center—remains in the planning stage.

1972 Plan

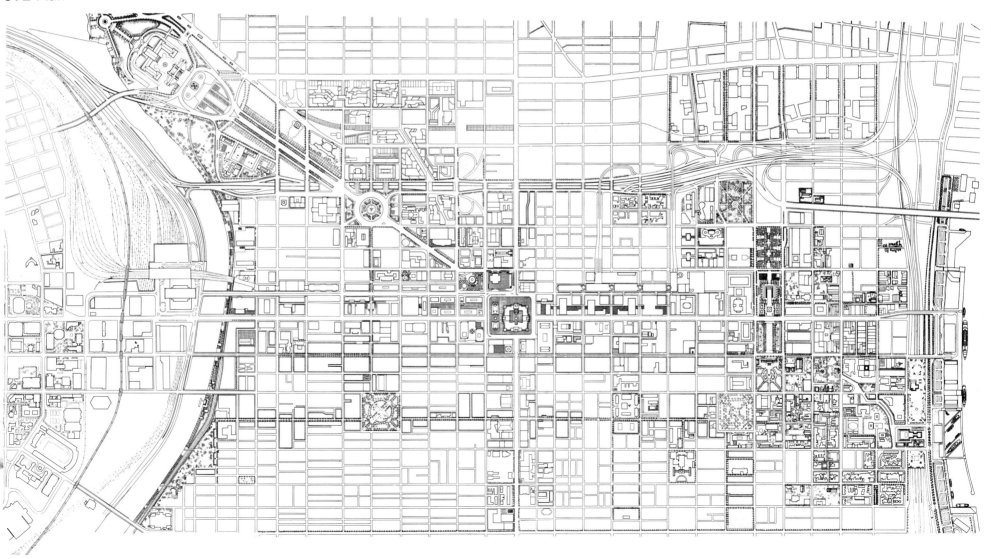

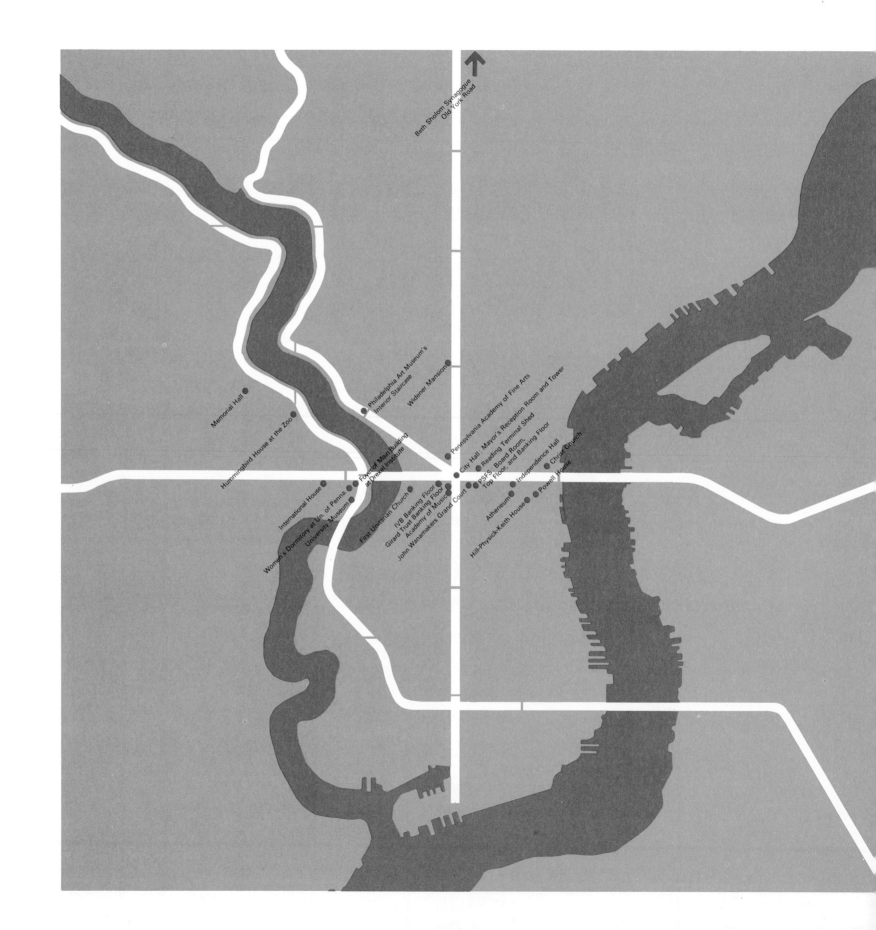

Memorial Hall

Philadelphia Art Museum's
Interior Staircase

Widener Mansion

Beth Sholom Synagogue
Old York Road

Pennsylvania Academy of Fine Arts

City Hall: Mayor's Reception Room and Tower

Reading Terminal Shed

Hummingbird House at the Zoo

Foyer of Main Building
at Drexel Institute

PSFS, Board Room,
Top Floor, and Banking Floor

Christ Church

Independence Hall

Powell House

International House

Women's Dormitory at Un. of Penna.

University Museum

First Unitarian Church

IVB Banking Floor

Girard Trust Banking Floor

Academy of Music

John Wanamakers Grand Court

Atheneum

Hill-Physick-Keith House

Most buildings are not designed to invite people to enter. Thus, with the exception of the obvious public buildings, few people see the interesting interiors throughout Philadelphia. In the historic area almost everyone views the Liberty Bell in Independence Hall, but more should view the exceptional residential interiors in Society Hill, only a few blocks away. While most homes in Society Hill are open only for house tours, the Bishop White House, Powel House, and Hill-Physick-Keith House have been well restored and are regularly open to the public. The interior of Christ Church and the upstairs reading room of the Atheneum, a fine example of nineteenth-century design, are in the same area.

The Philadelphia Museum of Art has an outstanding collection of interiors of other buildings; the Oriental rooms are outstanding. Of all the museums, the interior of the Pennsylvania Academy of Fine Arts is the most architecturally distinctive. The Academy of Music, recently restored, is one of the finest examples in the country of the traditional red-plush-and-gilt approach to concert hall design; its ballroom is modeled after the Hall of Mirrors at Versailles.

The rooms of City Hall should not be missed, for example, the Mayor's Reception Room, the ornate Supreme Court Room, and the Council Chamber, reputed to be the same size as the House of Lords in London. Nearby are several typically grandiose commercial interiors. The banking rooms of the Girard Bank, the First Pennsylvania, and the Fidelity Bank exemplify early twentieth-century commercial design. John Wanamaker Department Store is unique for its central grand court extending through the full nine stories of the building. It is filled with a variety of activities and displays including the largest organ in the world;

noon concerts are given daily. Two exceptional contemporary interiors are also in the immediate area: the plastic and flourescent banking room of the Industrial Valley Bank, one of the few strikingly modern interiors in the city, and the various rooms of the PSFS building. Though about thirty-nine years old, the PSFS interiors are still the finest and most consistent in design quality of any office building in the city. The banking room and the top-floor boardroom and terrace room are exceptional.

In West Philadelphia there are a few interesting interiors on the University of Pennsylvania campus. The skylighted court of Saarinen's Women's Dormitory (Hill Hall) is one; it is a pleasant place to have lunch. The first-floor interior arcade of International House and the domed Chinese Room and new wing of the University Museum are also exceptional. At Drexel University the interior court of the main building exemplifies

interior space designed for extensive public use. Nearby the Thirtieth Street Station of the Penn Central is one of the few remaining large, open (and somewhat barren) train stations built in the early part of this century.

Farther afield are the Widener Mansion (North Philadelphia), the many accurately restored houses of Fairmount Park (for which there are regular tours), and the traditional and contemporary houses in Germantown and Chestnut Hill (for which there are spring and fall tours.) At the zoo the Hummingbird House is a marvelous experience. Finally, in Elkins Park is Frank Lloyd Wright's Temple Beth Shalom. Inspired by the concept of the "lighted mountain," the temple has a glass pyramidal roof that allows natural light to flood the interior.

IVB, 17th and Market

Drexel Main Building, Chestnut and 32nd

PSFS Building, 12th and Market

Powel House, 24 South 3rd

Hill-Physick-Keith House, 4th and Delancey

Academy of Music, Broad and Locust

Mayor's Reception Room, City Hall

30th Street Station, 30th and Market

PSFS Bank, 12th and Market

Hill Hall, 34th and Walnut

International House, 36th and Chestnut

Christ Church, 2nd and Market

Philadelphia Art Museum, Great Hall and Staircase

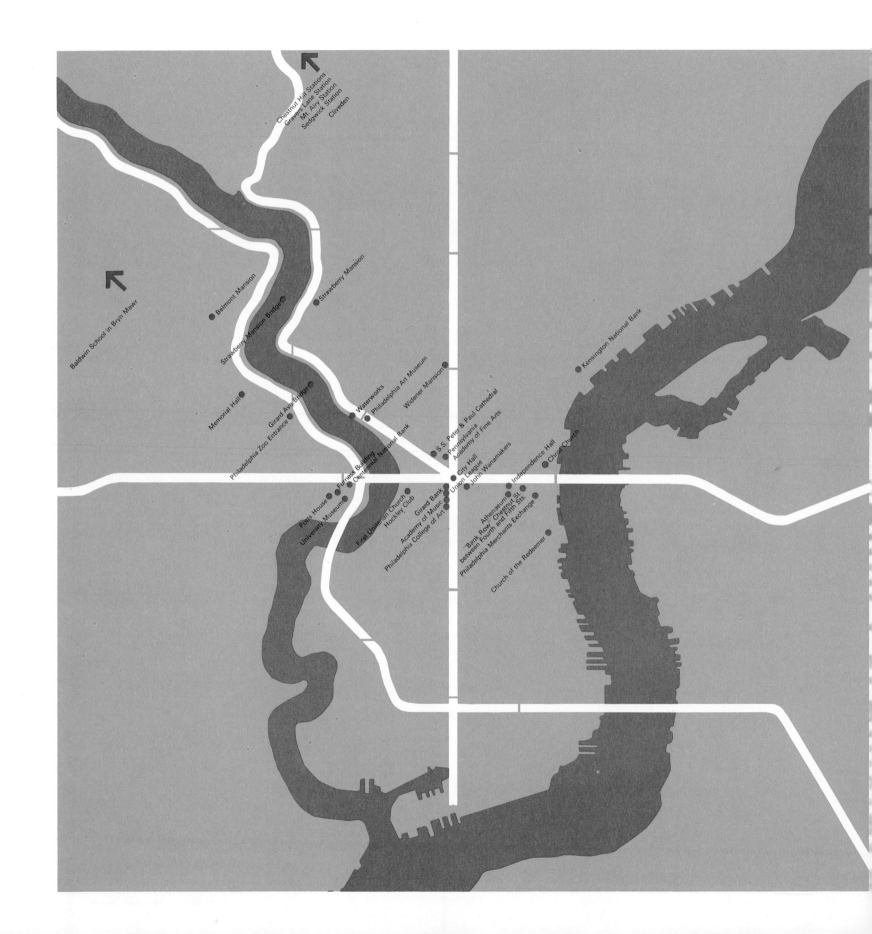

Chestnut Hill Stations:
Gravers Lane Station
Mt. Airy Station
Sedgwick Station
Cliveden

Belmont Mansion

Strawberry Mansion

Baldwin School in Bryn Mawr

Strawberry Mansion Bridge

Philadelphia Art Museum

Widener Mansion

Kensington National Bank

Memorial Hall

Waterworks

Girard Ave. Bridge

Philadelphia Zoo Entrance

S.S. Peter & Paul Cathedral

Pennsylvania
Academy of Fine Arts

Furness Building

Centennial National Bank

City Hall

Independence Hall

Christ Church

Pottš House

First Unitarian Church

Hockley Club

Girard Bank

Union League

John Wanamakers

University Museum

Academy of Music

Philadelphia College of Art

Athenaeum

"Bank Row," Chestnut St.
between Fourth and Fifth Sts.

Philadelphia Merchants Exchange

Church of the Redeemer

In colonial times buildings were designed by amateurs or by carpenters. Most early residential buildings were designed along the lines of English homes by their owners or builders and were required to meet limited functional requirements. The Slate Roof House (1700), formerly on Second Street, was one of the early brick houses that set the style for dwellings of the period. In the case of major buildings the designs were taken from books by the carpenters or other laymen and adapted to the purposes required.

The first real work of architecture in Philadelphia was Christ Church. It was started in 1727 and completed in 1774. James Hamilton is generally referred to as the "architect." Among its architectural distinctions is a grand Palladian-style window, first in the colonies. Other major projects that followed were similarly designed by the use of increasingly skillful adaptations of European buildings. Independence Hall, Mt. Pleasant in Fairmount Park, and the Pennsylvania Hospital were all designed in this manner.

The first professional architect in the present sense of the term was Benjamin Latrobe, designer of the houses along the northwest corner of Washington Square and of the first city waterworks. He was followed by William Strickland, who introduced classical styles in the Second Bank of the United States and the Merchants Exchange. His influence was carried on in the work of Robert Mills, John Haviland, and Thomas U. Walter, architect of Girard College and later of the Capitol in Washington, D.C.; all of these men practiced in Philadelphia at the same time. Strickland, Haviland, and Walter organized the Institute of Architects in 1836, which was the forerunner of the American Institute of Architects. The first architectural magazine, the Architectural Review and American Builders' Journal, was also started in Philadelphia (1868).

The most notable local architect of the latter nineteenth century was Frank Furness. Some examples of his work remain, although many have been demolished. The former Library of the University of Pennsylvania (now part of the Graduate School of Fine Arts) and the Pennsylvania Academy of Fine Arts are the best examples of his fertile eclecticism. During this period prominent outside architects, including Daniel Burnham (Wanamaker Store) and McKim, Mead and White (Girard Bank), began to do major projects in the city. Their neoclassical tradition and style were carried into the early part of the twentieth century by Horace Trumbauer (Philadelphia Art Museum) and Paul Cret.

The work of George Howe represents the transition to contemporary design. Howe designed a number of fine country houses in the partnership of Mellor, Meigs, and Howe, before turning his attention to his major achievement, the Philadelphia Savings Fund Society Building. Designed in partnership with William Lescaze, the PSFS building was the first modern building in the city and is still considered one of the most outstanding. At the end of his career Howe was a partner with Louis I. Kahn and Oscar Stonorov, and his work truly served as a bridge to present Philadelphia architecture.

Frank Furness

The most notable local architect of the latter nineteenth century was Frank Furness (1839-1912). A native Philadelphian, Furness received his early training in the New York office of Richard Morris Hunt. Returning to Philadelphia, Furness formed a partnership with George Hewitt, and in 1871 they received their first major commission, the Pennsylvania Academy of Fine Arts. Furness worked exclusively in Philadelphia, designing a number of significant commercial and civic structures (including the Old Broad Street Station of the Pennsylvania Railroad), almost all of which have been destroyed. The former Library of the University of Pennsylvania (now part of the Graduate School of Fine Arts) and the Pennsylvania Academy are the best remaining examples of his fertile eclecticism. Furness's influence was carried into contemporary architecture through one of his employees and students, Louis Sullivan, who was in turn the teach-teacher of Frank Lloyd Wright.

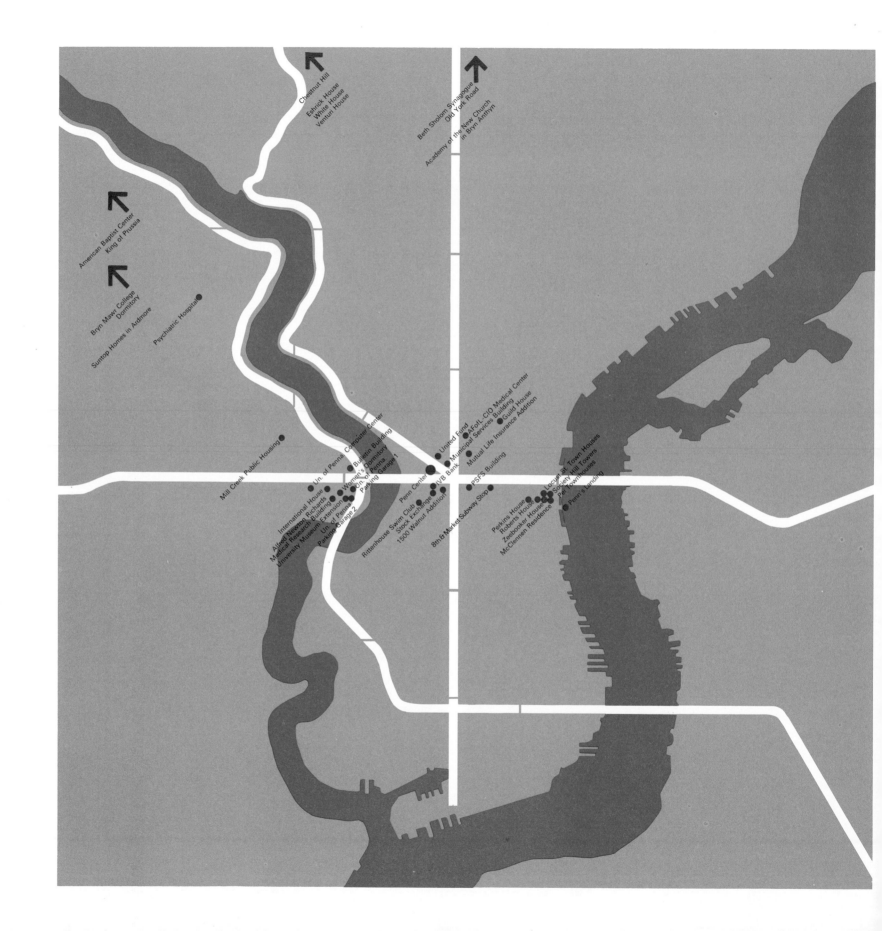

Chestnut Hill
Esbrick House
White House
Venturi House

Beth Sholom Synagogue
Old York Road
Academy of the New Church
in Bryn Athyn

American Baptist Center
King of Prussia

Bryn Mawr College
Dormitory
Suntop Homes in Ardmore
Psychiatric Hospital

United Fund
AFofL-CIO Medical Center
AFofL Services Building
Guild House
Mutual Life Insurance Addition

Mill Creek Public Housing

Un. of Penna Computer Center
Bulletin Building
Women's Dormitory
Un. of Penna
Parking Garage 1

Locust St. Town Houses
Society Hill Towers
Pei Townhouses
Penn's Landing

International House
Alfred Newton Richards
Medical Research Building
University Museum Extension
Un. of Penna
Parking Garage 2

Penn Center
IVB Bank
Municipal Services Building
PSFS Building

Rittenhouse Swim Club
Stock Exchange
1500 Walnut Addition
8th & Market Subway Stop

Perkins House
Roberts House
Zeebooker House
McClennen Residence

Present Philadelphia Architects

The resurgence of interest in the physical character of the city resulting from the Better Philadelphia Exhibit in 1947 provided an impetus to the developemnt of significant contemporary architecture. Even in areas such as Society Hill where historic restoration was dominant, design standards established by the City Planning Commission encouraged the use of contemporary forms and fostered the growth of an emerging architectural profession.

Urban renewal projects provided initial opportunities for many developing architectural firms. Master plans for Eastwick, Mill Creek, Penn's Landing, to name a few, led to specific residential projects. Mill Creek housing provided Louis I. Kahn with an early opportunity; East Falls public housing was one of the many housing projects designed by the late Oscar Stonorov; and the Society Hill Towers, one of several projects selected through national design competition, attracted non-Philadelphia architects such as I.M. Pei. Aided in its expansion by the urban renewal process, the University of Pennsylvania provided an opportunity for many prominent architects including Kahn, Eero Saarinen, Mitchell/Giurgola, and Richard Neutra.

In addition to urban renewal, the school rebuilding program, initiated under Richardson Dilworth's chairmanship, provided significant opportunities for public design. Several excellent schools resulted, of which Mitchell/Giurgola's William Penn High School for Girls is the most notable.

Public efforts led to a significant private response producing numerous outstanding houses in Society Hill and Chestnut Hill and a variety of commercial structures such as the United Fund Office Building on the Parkway.

The result of this extensive building program was a strengthened architectural profession in the city. The local American Institute of Architects (AIA) chapter became one of the strongest in the country and has been the initiator of three nationally significant programs. The AIA Workshop was founded in 1969 to provide design services to community groups who could not otherwise afford them. In 1970, with AIA sponsorship, the Group for Environment Education Inc. (GEE!) was established to develop a school curriculum and workbooks aimed at developing a broad awareness of the environment. Recently the AIA has been instrumental in establishing an interdisciplinary center for coordination of all the design and building professions in the city.

This organizational strength is a direct reflection of the development of many outstanding local firms, many of which have achieved national prominence. Preeminent among these is the firm of Louis I. Kahn. Born in Russia in 1901, Kahn attended the University of Pennsylvania, where he is now the Paul Cret Professor of Architecture. Well recognized for his teaching, Kahn received national attention as a result of the Richards Medical Building at the University of Pennsylvania, and his professional career has been further enhanced through such projects as the Salk Center in La Jolla, California. In 1971 he received the Gold Medal of the AIA as well as other international honors.

Kahn's presence drew many architects to the University of Pennsylvania and to the city, many of whom have also attained national reputations. In the field of urban design David A. Crane and David Wallace are the most prominent. Ian McHarg (in partnership with Wallace) has achieved an international reputation for his work in ecological and regional planning. Several other firms, such as Murphy Levy Wurman and Geddes, Brecker, Qualls, and Cunningham, have combined urban planning and architecture. Among the nationally prominent architectural firms are Mitchell/Giurgola Associates, Venturi and Rauch, Louis Sauer, and Vincent Kling.

In addition there are many excellent local firms whose work has been confined to the Philadelphia area, such as Bower and Fradley, and many young firms, such as Friday or Vollmer-Knowles, establishing their reputations through competitions.

The index is in three parts: A General Index, an Index of Buildings, and an Index of Architects. The General Index refers to the text, photographs, and general topics of maps and charts. The Index of Buildings and the Index of Architects both refer to map legends and provide a complete cross-referencing of <u>Man-Made Philadelphia</u> buildings (including dates of construction) and architects.

General Index

Page numbers in **medium** indicate photographs. Page numbers followed by the letter "m" indicate maps; those followed by "c" indicate charts.

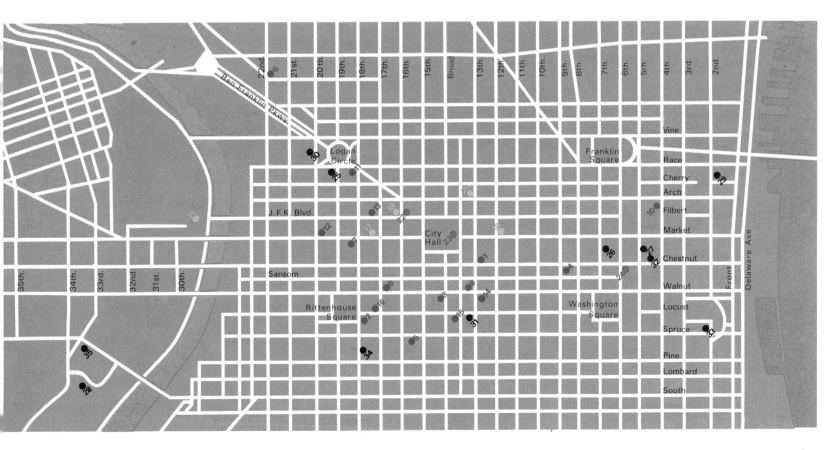

Index of Buildings

Philadelphia National Bank

Philadelphia Savings
Fund Society

Central Penn Bank

Industrial Valley Bank

Index of Architects

Air Pollution Complaints 686-5163
Bell Telephone Company
 Annoyance Calls 633-0050
 Business Offices 633-0050
 Executive Offices 466-9900
 Repair Service 611
City Hall 686-1776
Customs House 597-3311
Federal Bureau of Investigation 563-5300
Fire Department 563-6700
Health Department Administration Office
 686-1776
Help Inc. 546-7766 or 546-6925
Library, Logan Square 686-3990
Main Post Office 597-3311
Municipal Court 686-1776
Philadelphia Electric Company
 General Offices 841-4000
 Service and Repair 841-4141
Philadelphia Gas Works Emergency 236-7000
Philadelphia Rat Control Unit 472-2575
Poison Information Center 922-5523
Police Department 231-3131
Public Assistance Headquarters 238-7125
Snow and Storm Emergencies 686-4960
Streets Department 686-1776
Suicide Prevention Center 686-4420
Time 846-1212
Traffic Court 686-1776
Water Department Service and Complaints
 686-3900
Weather 936-1212
Western Union Telegrams 923-0500
Youth Study Center 686-1776

Airport Shuttle Service 726-5026
Greyhound Bus Lines 568-4800
Penn Central Metroliner 382-9015
Penn Central Trains 382-3030
Reading Railroad 922-6530
Salem Limousine Service 726-9955
SEPTA 329-4800
Trailways Bus Terminal 569-3100
United Cab Association 627-2225
Yellow Cab Company 922-8400

Allegheny Airlines 568-7103
Altair Airlines 726-1800
American Airlines 568-3600
Braniff Airlines 925-9476
Continental Airlines 925-4252
Delta Airlines 928-1700
Eastern Airlines 923-3500
National Airlines 923-1860
Northwest Airlines 922-2900
Pan American World Airways 569-1300
Suburban Airlines 800-422-8175
Trans World Airlines 923-2000
United Airlines 568-2800

Philadelphia Inquirer 563-1600
Philadelphia Bulletin 382-7600
Philadelphia Daily News 563-5200

Academy of Music 735-7379
Academy of Natural Sciences 564-3921
American Institute of Architects 569-3186
Arena 386-1500
Board of Education 448-3800
Bureau of Immigration and Naturalization
 569-7312
Free Library of Philadelphia 686-3990
Franklin Institute 564-3838
Historical Society of Pennsylvania 732-6200
Pennsylvania Academy of Fine Arts 564-0219
Philadelphia Chamber of Commerce 735-9320
Philadelphia Civic Center Museum 686-1776
Philadelphia Museum of Art 763-8100
Philadlephia Tourist Bureau 561-1200
Philadelphia Veterans Stadium 463-5300
Philadelphia Zoo 222-5300
Spectrum 389-5000
Ticketron 546-8100
University Museum 386-7400

104

Bibliography

Guidebooks

Philadelphia Guide by Nancy Love (published by Philadelphia Magazine, 1972) and the Collegiate Guide to Greater Philadelphia (published by Mixed Media, Inc., 1972) both provide comprehensive information about activities in the Philadelphia area. The Collegiate Guide has an extensive section on restaurants and their quality and prices, and the Philadelphia Guide has a series of well-described short tours of areas of primary interest to visitors. Though not exactly a guidebook, the Bulletin Almanac, edited by Isadore Lichstein (The Philadelphia Evening and Sunday Bulletin, 1972) contains the most extensive collection of facts available about Philadelphia and the surrounding area.

Public Documents

The Tourist and Convention Bureau (John F. Kennedy Boulevard at Seventeenth Street) and other local organizations provide a wide variety of pamphlets, maps, and tours of interesting places and events in the Philadelphia area. The Philadelphia City Planning Commission regularly publishes updated plans of the city and other items of public interest. These include A List of Notable Buildings in Philadelphia, Center City Walking Tour (which includes Society Hill), and Population and Housing Statistics and Trends (1970 Census). The Delaware Valley Regional Planning Commission does the same thing at a regional level and recently published an Inventory of Historic Sites (1970). In general, these are available without cost.

References

Many books have been written on the physical and social growth of Philadelphia. George Tatum's Penn's Great Town (University of Pennsylvania Press, 1961) and Historic Germantown by Harry and Margaret Tinkum and Grant Simon (the American Philosophical Society, 1955) are both concerned with the development of Philadelphia architecture. Two excellent sources on city history are The Private City: Philadelphia in Three Periods of Its Growth by Sam B. Warner, Jr. (University of Pennsylvania Press, 1970), and Historic Philadelphia, Transactions of the American Philosophical Society (Vol. 43, Part 1), which covers the period from the founding until the early nineteenth century and contains a fascinating series of monographs on both physical and social development. An Illustrated History of the Centennial by James D. McCabe (National Publishing Co., 1876) contains a very detailed description of the principal parts of the city as they appeared at that time.

All of these sources were published in Philadelphia.

Acknowledgments

Many individuals made significant contributions to the development of this book during the several years of its preparation.

Considerable assistance was provided by the Philadelphia City Planning Commission. R. Damon Childs, Executive Director, reviewed both the orginazation of the book and the accuracy of the text and mapped information. Alfred Tolzer, Chief of Social Planning, was principally responsible for the sections on population growth and distribution. Alois Strobl, Joseph McLaughlin, and Robert Presser developed the population and street maps that accompany those sections.

The initial architectural photographs were provided by George Krause. Additional photographs and creative assistance were provided by Howard Brunner, Valerie Pettis, John Ellis, and Stephan Geissbuhler. Gene Feldman of the Falcon Press was helpful in advising on early production problems. Special thanks are due to Howard Brunner of Murphy Levy Wurman who was responsible for the final graphic layout and the laborious notations.

Nancy Love read the text on several occasions and gave invaluable editorial assistance, as did Alan Halpern. Frank Calsmer was responsible for the index.

About the Book

Man's most complex inventions are his cities. Understanding them is a difficult task at best. Man-Made Philadelphia is a special kind of key to the city because it goes beyond a listing of places for visitors. This book is a key to Philadelphia which unlocks the city to understanding and discovery—allowing us to see the things we always see but never see. And uniquely, it is a guide for visitors and residents alike.

This is a guide to a city full of experiences as well as places. Far more than an annotated map of a city with historical significance, this book provides a comprehensive view of Philadelphia as a city with interrelated parts that are constantly changing, growing, and sometimes being planned. Where individual buildings and monuments are highlighted, special attention has been paid to depicting these in their larger human settings with a sensitivity to their place in the total environment of the city.

Profusely illustrated with 176 exceptional photographs and 105 specially designed colored maps and map overlays, the text provides an image of Philadelphia as it is seen by citizens and visitors as they drive along its major routes or walk within its distinctive, largely homogeneous areas. Man-Made Philadelphia is a guide to a city as it really is. With obvious fondness for their city, the authors have presented the details of its beauty marks and warts and all.

The reader is oriented along the major routes—Market and Broad, the Benjamin Franklin Parkway and the Schuylkill Expressway. He is guided through a number of areas, including Independence Mall, Franklin and Washington and Rittenhouse squares, Logan Circle, Society Hill, University City, Fairmount Park, Penn Center, Germantown, and Chestnut Hill.

The process by which the city has evolved and continues to change is vividly presented through thoughtful graphic material depicting population changes, ethnic patterns, legal jurisdictions, and political districts. And, at last, a special gift—a map of the transportation networks with which we can actually wend our way from where we are to where we would like to be. In reality this is the proverbial "key to the city" which, though often talked about, is seldom provided.

Man-Made Philadelphia is significant because it suggests a prototypical means of city description. Written by two architect-urban planners for the average visitor or resident, it reflects a depth of understanding seldom captured in such easy to understand terms.

If Philadelphia merits a book like this, it is also true that this book is worthy of Philadelphia.

Every guidebook is a particularly oriented slice of information about a city. Some slices available from the MIT Press are the following titles:

Boston/Architecture
Boston Society of Architects

Guide to Cambridge Architecture:
Ten Walking Tours
Robert Bell Rettig

Making the City Observable
Richard Saul Wurman

Urban Atlas:
20 American Cities
Joseph R. Passonneau and Richard Saul Wurman

Aspen Visible
Joel Katz and Richard Saul Wurman

Yellow Pages of Learning Resources
Richard Saul Wurman, editor

Our Man-Made Environment
Book Seven
GEE! Group for Environmental Education Inc.

Le Cadre de Vie Oeuvre de l'homme
GEE! Group for Environmental Education Inc.

The MIT Press
Massachusetts Institute of Technology
Cambridge, Massachusetts 02142

Notes on the Authors

Richard Saul Wurman is a partner in the firm of Murphy Levy Wurman, Architecture and Urban Planning, in Philadelphia. A graduate of the University of Pennsylvania, Mr. Wurman has been on the faculties of City College of New York, Cambridge University, Princeton University, and North Carolina State University. He has received a Graham Fellowship, a Chandler Fellowship, and a Guggenheim Fellowship. Some of his publications include Making the City Observable (Design Quarterly 80); Urban Atlas: 20 American Cities (with Joseph Passonneau); The Notebooks and Drawings of Louis I. Kahn (with Eugene Feldman); The City: Form and Intent; Various Dwellings Described in a Comparative Manner; Yellow Pages of Learning Resources; and Aspen Visible (with Joel Katz). He created a show on the public environment, City/2, for the Philadelphia Museum of Art and is a board member of the International Design Conference in Aspen. Mr. Wurman is Vice President and Secretary of GEE!, Group for Environmental Education, Inc.

John Andrew Gallery is a graduate of Harvard College and the Harvard University Graduate School of Design. He has been active in public urban development in Philadelphia for a number of years first on the staff of the Philadelphia City Planning Commission, and subsequently as Executive Director of the Philadelphia 1976 Bicentennial Corporation, where he was responsible for the development of initial plans for an International Exposition in Philadelphia in 1976. Currently Mr. Gallery is a visiting professor in the Urban Design Studio of the University of Pennsylvania.

Legend

- Reading Company
- Penn Central Company
- Septa
- Port Authority Transit Company
- ○ Interchange with same line
- ◉ Interchange with different line

To Bethlehem — To Doylestown — To New York

Elm St.
Main St.
Norristown
To Reading and Pottsville

Perkasie, Sellersville, Telford, Souderton, Hatfield, Lansdale, Pennbrook, North Wales, Gwynedd Valley, Penllyn, Ambler, Fort Washington, Fellwick, Oreland, North Hills, Glenside

Link Belt, Colmar, Fortuna

Holland, Churchville, Southampton, County Line, Bryn Athyn, Huntingdon Valley, Philmont, Bethayres, Rydal, Noble, Meadowbrook, Ardsley

West Trenton, Yardley, Woodbourne, Fairless Junction, Langhorne, Parkland, Neshaminy Falls, Trevose, Somerton, Forest Hills

Hatboro, Fulmor, Willow Grove, Crestmont, Roslyn

Walnut Hill, Fox Chase, Ryers, Cheltenham, Lawndale, Crescentville

Bridgeport, King Manor, Hughes Park, Gulph Mills, Conshohocken Rd., County Line, Radnor, Villanova Station, Villanova Stadium, Garrett Hill, Rosemont, Bryn Mawr, Haverford, Ardmore Ave., Ardmore Jct., Wynnewood

Mogees, Ivy Rock, Conshohocken, Spring Mill, Miquon, Shawmont, Manayunk, Wissahickon, East Falls

Chestnut Hill, Highland, St. Martins, Allens Lane, Carpenter, Upsal, Tulpehocken, Chelten Ave., Queen Lane, Westmoreland

Gravers, Wyndmoor, Mt. Airy, Sedgwick, Stenton, Washington Lane, Germantown, Wister, Fishers, Wayne Junction, Nicetown, Tioga

Fernrock, Olney, Logan, Wyoming, Hunting Park, Erie, Allegheny

Elkins Park, Melrose Park, Fernrock, Tabor, Logan, Olney

Bridge-Pratt, Margaret-Orthodox, Church, Erie-Torresdale, Tioga, Allegheny, Somerset

Trenton, Levittown-Tullytown, Bristol, Croydon, Eddington, Cornwells Heights, Andalusia, Torresdale, Holmesburg Junction, Tacony, Wissinoming, Bridesburg, Frankford, Frankford Junction

North Philadelphia, Huntingdon, Susquehanna-Dauphin, Columbia, Girard, Fairmount, Spring Garden, Race-Vine, Suburban

North Broad St., Temple University, Dauphin-York, Berks, Girard, Fairmount, Spring Garden St.

Barmouth, Cynwd, Bala, Wynnefield Ave.

Villanova, Rosemont, Bryn Mawr, Haverford, Ardmore, Wynnewood, Narberth, Merion, Overbrook

Beachwood, Brookline, Market-Frankford Line

Penfield, West Overbrook, Parkview, 69th St., Milbourne, 63rd St., 60th St., 56th St., 52nd St., 49th St., 46th St., 40th St., 33rd St., Sansom St., 37th St.

52nd St., 34th St., 30th St., 22nd St., 19th St., 15th St., Walnut-Locust, 13th St., 11th St., 8th St., 5th St., 2nd St.

8th & Vine, City Hall-Camden, Broadway-Camden, Ferry Ave.

Philadelphia-Lindenwold Line, Collingswood, Westmont, Haddonfield, Ashland, Lindenwold, Pennsylvania-Reading Seashore Line

City Hall, Reading Terminal, Broad St. Subway

Lombard-South, Ellsworth-Federal, Tasker-Morris, Snyder, Oregon, Pattison

12th-13th Locust, 9th-10th Locust

Media Line, Sharon Hill Line, Angora, Fernwood, Lansdowne, Gladstone, Clifton, Primos, Secane, Morton, Swarthmore, Wallingford

Darby, Curtis Park, Sharon Hill, Folcroft, Glenolden, Norwood

To Media, To Media and West Chester, To Wilmington, To Radnor and Paoli, Wynnewood

Haddonfield, Ashland, Hammonton, Egg Harbor, Absecon, Atlantic City, Tuckahoe

To New York, To Cape May, To Ocean City

Schuylkill River, Delaware River

12-100